Understanding the Human Mind

Murderous Thoughts

Jason Browne

© Copyright 2021 - All rights reserved.

The content contained within this book may not be reproduced, duplicated or transmitted without direct written permission from the author or the publisher.

Under no circumstances will any blame or legal responsibility be held against the publisher, or author, for any damages, reparation, or monetary loss due to the information contained within this book, either directly or indirectly.

Legal Notice:

This book is copyright protected. It is only for personal use. You cannot amend, distribute, sell, use, quote or paraphrase any part, or the content within this book, without the consent of the author or publisher.

Disclaimer Notice:

Please note the information contained within this document is for educational and entertainment purposes only. All effort has been executed to present accurate, up to date, reliable, complete information. No warranties of any kind are declared or implied. Readers acknowledge that the author is not engaged in the rendering of legal, financial, medical or professional advice. The content within this book has been derived from various sources. Please consult a licensed professional before attempting any techniques outlined in this book.

By reading this document, the reader agrees that under no circumstances is the author responsible for any losses, direct or indirect, that are incurred as a result of the use of the information contained within this document, including, but not limited to, errors, omissions, or inaccuracies.

Table of Contents

TABLE OF CONTENTS 5

INTRODUCTION 1

CHAPTER 1: WHAT EXACTLY IS A PSYCHOPATH AND WHAT ARE THEIR TRAITS? 7
- Aberrant People 8
- Birth or Design 11
- Identifiable Traits 17

CHAPTER 2: INSIDE THE BRAIN OF A PSYCHOPATH 23
- The Mind of a Psychopath 23
- The Hidden Suffering of Psychopaths 27
- What Drives Their Selfishness? 31
- Clues You're Dealing With a Psychopath 34

CHAPTER 3: PSYCHOPATHS AROUND YOU 39
- Recognizing a Psychopath 39
- Relative Impact 45
- Investigating Closer Relationships 49
  - *Friendly Suspects* 49
  - *Parenting a Monster* 53
  - *Dating a Psychopath* 54

CHAPTER 4: PSYCHOPATH VERSUS SOCIOPATH 59
- Distinguishing Similarities 59
- The Creation of Each 63
- Diagnosing Primary and Secondary Psychopathy 65
- Distinct Differences 68

CHAPTER 5: HOW PSYCHOPATHS SEE THE WORLD - CAN YOU CHANGE THEM? 73

Through the Eyes of a Psychopath 74
Is Change Possible? 80

CHAPTER 6: HOW TO DEAL WITH PSYCHOPATHS AND THEIR WEAKNESSES 87

Three Mental Fortes 88
Watch Out! 90
Five Secrets of Dealing With Psychopaths 97

CHAPTER 7: ARE ALL PSYCHOPATHS CRIMINALS? 103

Classical Versus Successful Psychopathy 104
Functional Psychopaths 108
Murderers and Psychopaths 112

CHAPTER 8: AM I A PSYCHOPATH? 119

Psychopathy Test 119
Self-Assessment for Psychopathy 125
Considering Facts 128

CONCLUSION 135

REFERENCES 139

Introduction

Robert D. Hare once said, "A psychopath can use the words 'I love you,' but it means nothing more to him than if he said 'I'll have a cup of coffee.'" Staring into the eyes of a psychopath while they express themselves superficially is like staring down a wall and believing the words you see written on it as though the inanimate object spoke to you. Have you ever truly looked into a psychopath's eyes? Think about the infamous photos of John Wayne Gacy, Ted Bundy, and Jeffrey Dahmer. Nothing can make your skin crawl more than the dead eyes of a serial killer. Their words have no tonality, and they speak matter-of-factly, even about the most mortifying crimes they have committed. Just imagine for one moment that you're telling someone about how you sliced and diced someone else. Cringeworthy is an understatement.

Whenever we think of psychopaths, we tend to conjure images in our minds of the men and women who did the unthinkable. However, this isn't the true face of a modern psychopath. Once you know the truth about psychopaths and how their minds work, you may start questioning whether your friends, colleagues, and relatives are psychopathic. It's a fair question to ponder because the main focus surrounding psychopaths has always been on serial killers and rapists. Sometimes, it goes beyond murdering people. Jeffrey Dahmer was the infamous Milwaukee Cannibal who ate his victims. The things some humans are capable of are unfathomable to say the least. History tells us to fear psychopaths. It tells us to question why we have murderous thoughts because something may be wrong.

Who does a psychopath turn to when murderous thoughts pop into their minds? They aren't always taken seriously by the large number of people who think a psychopath is someone who kills, rapes, and keeps trophies. Only a small portion of the world knows what a true psychopath is and where they hide. Fortunately, this number is growing because psychopaths are hiding in plain sight and better research is exposing them. Some of them are stationed in powerful positions because they're unemotional and relentless drones. They don't allow silly things like emotions to deter them from their goals. Some psychopaths are well-trusted individuals, albeit we sometimes suspect that not all their gears are in place. The fact is that a psychopath is probably the person you least expect them to be.

They camouflage themselves like chameleons, even though they leave a trail of disaster and wounded people in their wake. Ask yourself why you're here right now. You've probably crossed a psychopath, been hurt by one, or you suspect yourself to be a psychopathic individual. Curiosity piqued for some people to learn what a true psychopath looks like, and hopefully, you learn to avoid these kinds of people before you become a victim. Psychopaths have numerous subtler ways of hurting the people with whom they interact. Their inability to feel emotions the way normal people do can make them dangerous people to be associated with. Perhaps you worry that your child shows signs of psychopathic behavior, and all you want as a parent is to lead them down a different path. You can't imagine seeing them in prison one day.

Maybe your encounter with a psychopath has been in the romantic plain, or perhaps you're suspicious of someone at work. The eerie truth is that you not only encounter multiple psychopaths in your lifetime, but you may even encounter them daily without knowing it (Barker, 2016). The reason psychopaths are so misunderstood is that research has focused too long on the violent criminals locked up in our prisons. This is finally changing though. Psychopathy is now recognized as a disorder that may affect more people than we could imagine. These people are referred to as functional or successful, but it doesn't mean we mustn't watch out for them.

One study published by the Virginia Commonwealth University might open new doors to understanding how some psychopaths function as well as regular people do, if not better (McNeill, 2020). At one point, it would've been considered madness to believe some psychopaths live among us, never being caught because they have an advantage over criminal psychopaths. However, neuroscience is proving that they exist. Knowing how sly, unapologetic, unethical, immoral, emotionless, and ruthless a psychopath is capable of being confirms why people should learn more about them. This could help people protect themselves and their loved ones. It can even help you recognize someone in your family or social circle who has the potential to harm you.

Their harm won't always come in a physical form. A psychopath can ruin you emotionally if you aren't sure how to manage your interactions with them. Even if you suspect yourself as a psychopath, or you just want to know if you're overthinking things because of media sensationalism and negativity, you'll benefit from knowing what a psychopath looks like. You need to know what makes them psychopathic and how this can manifest itself to hurt the people around this person. To protect your loved ones and yourself, you need to delve into the science behind psychopaths. Their brain activity looks nothing like a normal person's activity, and that explains why they can be so callous and remorseless. You must learn about the different types of psychopaths and whether it's nature or nurture that designs them.

You'll be able to recognize them by their traits and disarm their superficial and sly charm used to attract people. Psychopaths have common vulnerabilities they target, and you can stop them from doing this with a little knowledge and proven tactics. Moreover, you'll know why their personality can charm the shoes off your feet. Manipulation is their game. Some psychopaths can also slide their way into government agencies, religious organizations, and executive positions. You must know why they can do this compared to the psychopaths filling our prisons. The most dangerous psychopaths aren't found in prison. They're found where you least expect them to be. You'll have questions you can use to determine whether you or a friend is psychopathic, and then you'll learn how to embrace this shocking truth.

You'll also know how to recognize whether your child is a psychopath, and you'll know what you can do to prevent them from becoming the next Jack the Ripper. Psychopaths and sociopaths are also different types of people, and you'll learn what the latest research says about what differentiates them. What may be the most pressing curiosity about psychopathy that has everyone edging their seats is whether they can be changed, treated, or improved. This question isn't simple to answer, but some promising research proves whether this can or can't be done. Whatever the outcome, whomever you recognize as a psychopath, you'll have five methods to deal with them so you don't become their next victim. Finally, you can use the underrated psychopathy checklist to determine if you're one.

Some disorders are depressing, and others are unexplainable, but psychopathy is neither thanks to the research being done. Psychopathy is a dangerous disorder, and the best chance you have of not being the next victim is to unravel the secrets behind the personality dysfunction. I've long had an interest in the human mind, hence the series of books. I spend countless hours studying the inner-working of the mind to understand disorders myself. My love for unraveling the human mind and brain stems from curiosity, but combined with my education, it can open gateways for people who need the knowledge. It doesn't matter if you're just interested in learning more or you want to understand something that deeply disturbs you; sharing my passion with you matters deeply to me.

Beyond my passion, I also have been unfortunate to encounter psychopaths. My experience led me to research this particular disorder because the internet doesn't pack everything neatly in a bundle for us. It takes months or years to find correlations between a specific disorder and what the current data reveals. Most importantly, I don't want anyone else to suffer at the hands of a psychopath. The information you're about to uncover has helped me protect my family and loved ones from the indescribable dangers posed by a psychopath. To defend yourself against an enemy, you must know the enemy better than you know yourself. If you are the enemy, you must know what you are so you can benefit from your dysfunctional way of thinking.

Anyone, even yourself, could be living with or next to a psychopath. You could be working with one daily, or you may even work for one. Your partner could be a psychopath, and so can your child. Not knowing what exactly a psychopath is can pose a danger to your life, health, and success. If you're ready to uncover the face of a true psychopath, then it's time for you to dive into the first chapter.

Chapter 1:

What Exactly Is a Psychopath and What Are Their Traits?

Names like Ted Bundy and John Wayne Gacy often spring to mind when you think about psychopaths. You might even remember Adolf Hitler, who certainly was psychopathic by all definitions. It's common for your mind to wander off to the first name that made news or history because these men were anything but normal. However, serial killers and mass murderers aren't the only psychopaths in this world. For all you know, your neighbor, friend, or boss could be a psychopath, and you won't be safe until you know what their bizarre traits look like. They don't think the way you do, so learn to recognize them, even if you're one yourself.

Aberrant People

We loosely use the terms psychopathy and sociopathy, but these names aren't included in the formal database of mental disorders. You can call these terms a layman way of generalizing people who don't fit into the norms of society. These people seem awkward, manipulative, and dangerous, and you're right in some cases, but psychopaths aren't always as blatantly dangerous as you think. Psychopathy can be as subtle as a gentle breeze passing for days before a hurricane, and some psychopaths never become a hurricane. If meteorologists waited for the winds to change before declaring a warning over the news, we'd be in pretty deep waters—pun intended. What you can know is that not every aberrant person will become dangerous, and not every dangerous person is a psychopath.

Both psychopaths and sociopaths are just names we use, but neither of these terms is a condition in itself. Psychopathy is not a mental disorder, but the true name for this condition is antisocial personality disorder (ASPD), according to psychiatrist Prakash Masand (Lindberg & Legg, 2019). ASPD can refer to psychopathy or sociopathy, which are slightly different. You'll learn about this in Chapter Four. Under the umbrella of ASPD, some similarities between the two conditions are having a manipulative nature and being capable of violating other people's well-being, happiness, boundaries, and morals. People often get confused by the word 'antisocial.' If you're imagining someone who behaves awkwardly around social gatherings, you're wrong.

The antisocial factor in the personality disorder means psychopaths have no regard for other people's rights. They'll behave in a way that goes against societal rules, norms, laws, and morals. In this sense, psychopaths are deeply narcissistic and self-centered. They'll always consider their own progress above anyone else's, even if it causes problems for other people. Antisocial means that psychopaths go against what society considers normal behavior in this disorder. Psychopaths also have little to no conscience when it comes to promoting themselves in work, relationships, or the community at the cost of other people. They'll hurt, manipulate, or use you to gain a better standing. They have a problem with emotional control, and they're unemotional in severe cases.

Psychopaths might disregard acceptable and responsible behavior so much that they even behave irresponsibly toward themselves, opening themselves to danger. Psychopaths are reckless and deceitful, but they're superficially charming. Their charm is guided by selfishness and manipulative intentions, especially with people outside of their inner community. Psychopaths can also be extremely aggressive, or a milder psychopath might express a short temper. Aberrant people can also lack remorse for their behaviors, and they can be impulsive, abusive, and violent. Their violence knows no bounds because they are mentally and physically violent in some cases.

Masand also explains that psychopathy is more common among men, and it's normally diagnosed after the age of 18. Some children will show signs of abnormal misconduct by 11, but they're diagnosed as having conduct disorder (CD) or oppositional defiant disorder (ODD). Both of these childhood disorders share the same traits as psychopathy. Children go against the grain of society, and their recurrent behavior is outside of normal expectations. They also show no remorse or empathy. CD is the more severe form of childhood antisocial personality behavior. Anyway, ASPD is a serious mental disorder, but it should be said again, it's not always severe like the serial killers you watch on reality television. It can be subtler, and you'll only truly recognize the potential for the disorder if you're aware of the common traits.

Treating ASPD is also challenging. Mental healthcare workers or psychotherapists will usually treat someone with ASPD with a combination of medication and psychotherapy. Medication merely treats the underlying symptoms of the disorder because you can't treat someone's personality per se. The medication might target aggressiveness or impulsivity, but psychotherapy is more commonly used to help psychopaths recognize how their disorder affects their lives. The bottom line is that psychopathy is a misinformed term often used by the general public. It can confuse what you should be looking for. Understanding the precept behind the antisocial factor of the disorder is what can help you recognize it within others or yourself.

Birth or Design

The question of nature versus nurture is relevant in every mental disorder. Understanding how psychopaths come to be can help us distinguish who is more likely to become one. It's also monumentally important to establish the answer because psychopaths tend to use their suffering as a crutch by which they manipulate you. Psychopathy or ASPD is a disorder that lasts a lifetime once it shows itself, and it's characterized by someone who has a complete disregard for other people's human rights. They also have little to no morals or ethics, and the absence of the level of conscience most people possess can be dangerous. Still, we keep thinking of the serial killer archetypes, but that's a rare truth. Some psychopaths function better and more intelligently than most people, and they become great success stories.

What might seem disturbing about psychopathy is that regular societies want to understand them by watching endless shows, reading books, and rehashing the movies made about these famously notorious men. On one hand, this is great because it helps us remain safe. On the other hand, it shows that people love watching reality shows about the sickest minds in the world. Rest assured, keeping yourself and your loved ones safe matters more than questioning your reason for wanting more information. It's perfectly normal to want to know more when it can help you control your tendencies or protect yourself from a psychopath.

Humans will always be curious. It doesn't make them psychopaths.

This same level of curiosity is what allows scientists and psychotherapists to study the mind of psychopaths so we can know if they were born this way or if their parents made them aberrant. So, how do people become psychopaths? Genetics has a role in psychopathy. It starts with the evolution of man. Historically, humans had to defend themselves against danger, and resources were quite limited. These two factors could be the first reason why these genes were passed down from primitive humans to us today. We don't all contain this incredible selfishness and defensiveness, but some people are genetically predisposed to be more selfish than others. A hint of narcissism can be beneficial to your progress in life, but an overbearing sense of self and uncontrolled aggressiveness to feed the self are not normal in any sense.

A psychopath's brain also works differently, which makes geneticists believe nature has a hand in psychopathy (Delgado, 2020). Scans have shown how the structure of a psychopath's brain differs from a regular person's. They seem to lack the functionality to support impulse control, behavioral regulation, and emotional perception. A normal person's brain is capable of understanding and trying to imitate someone else's emotional facial cues. This happens beneath our awareness. The brain can latch onto certain facial cues you aren't even paying attention to, and the brain will automatically try to console the person with an imitated, empathetic response in your facial muscles. Psychopaths don't have this ability. In fact, when asked to draw emotional faces, psychopaths draw hardly any differences between anger, happiness, fear, or guilt.

However, these tell-tale signs of genetic and structural differences in a psychopath's brain don't guarantee that they'll become psychopathic. Some people are genetically predisposed to psychopathy, but they'll never become one. A genetic predisposition is necessary to determine whether someone will become a psychopath, but those who become the famous faces we know today might have more than a genetic pivot. Psychopathy is considered to be enhanced by various factors, and the more a psychopath can relate to the factors, the more probable they'll become a severe ASPD sufferer. Nature and nurture will determine your risk for becoming a psychopath as it determined Ted Bundy's outcome. Fortunately, severe psychopaths are only estimated to include one percent of the world's population (Choi, 2009).

One study conducted by the University of Minnesota suggests that genetics play an important role in psychopathy (Blonigen et al., 2005). The study included 626 pairs of twins who were all 17 at the time. The psychopathic traits were recorded using a multidimensional personality questionnaire. The university also used structural equation modeling to record the genetic and environmental influences patterns of each participant. This is a mathematical method used to determine genetic predisposition. The participants were then divided into two groups, namely those with fearless dominance traits or those with impulsive antisociality traits.

Fearless dominance is an internal form of psychopathy where recklessness and self-centeredness are most prevalent. Impulsive antisociality is an external form of psychopathy where the lack of responsibility and care for other people's rights is disregarded entirely. The impulsive antisociality group who showed genetic predispositions were more likely to become dangerous and callous. What the study from the University of Minnesota proved though is that some higher genetic contributions are more influential in psychopathy. The higher the prevalence of genes was in the twins, the more likely they were to display impulsive antisociality traits. This concludes that the number of predisposing genes can determine the severity of psychopathy.

Perpetua Neo is a specialist in dark triad personalities. Neo confirms that our evolution and genetic inheritance shouldn't be underestimated (Dodgson, 2017). Genetic evolution doesn't care whether you're a good person deep down or not, and it intends to hand you genes it feels are more likely suited to the environment in which you live. A psychopath can't avoid having the traits, but they can learn to recognize them so they can avoid being dominated by their genetic baseline. Fortunately, Neo also explains that your genetic heritage isn't the ultimate determining factor in your life. Various genes can also express themselves differently in various people, and this is sometimes affected by the environment. Behavior can be learned, rewarded, and reinforced, especially in childhood.

If your parents were manipulative and selfish, chances are you'll gain more than just their genes. You may gain their lack of empathy toward other people because your attitude is also learned. An interesting study was published in the *European Journal of Psychotraumatology* (Craparo et al., 2013). Twenty-two violent Italian offenders were examined to look for environmental similarities. Fourteen of the men were murderers, four were rapists, and four were child sex offenders. A standardized psychopathy test was used to measure their levels of psychopathy, and this was compared to their childhoods. Two of the main similarities among the offenders were childhood neglect and abuse. The offenders who rated the highest on the test for psychopathy were also found to have experienced social childhood trauma.

Severe or violent psychopathy may be related to childhood trauma, post-traumatic stress disorder (PTSD), and the big T traumas that abusively threatened their lives or quality of life as children. Childhood experiences is the largest environmental factor in psychopathy. Emotional abuse, whether it's intended by the parents or not, can also play a role in developing psychopathy, and so can emotional neglect or feelings of abandonment. A study published in *Psychological Medicine* examined abandonment issues in relation to psychopathy (Gao et al., 2010). Bonding with your parents during early childhood should never be underestimated. The study focused on children who were separated from their parents before they turned three. The disruption in the parental bonding in abandoned children caused them to have higher psychopathic scores at 28.

A child younger than three even feels abandoned when their parents get divorced. Children's minds are so impressionable, and it can lead to unwanted outcomes when the child already has a genetic predisposition to psychopathy. However, psychopaths are already wired to think and behave in certain ways because of their genetic inheritance. In some cases, parental influence and the childhood environment can't be the cause of the severity of psychopathy. Some children are innately designed to be evil. Have you ever heard of a child who dissects their puppy just for the heck of it? Maybe you used to kick your kitten around because you felt powerful compared to this small animal? Children can also be psychopathic, and sadly, it can become severe at a young age, meaning that genetics is the main contributing factor.

One disturbing case of a child gone dark was published in the *Atlantic* (Hagerty, 2017). 'Samantha' is the name used to protect the child's identity, but her story is hair-raising. Samantha created a book about violently hurting people by the time she was six. Her book was something from a horror story, and it included images of weapons and notes on how to suffocate someone. She had poison, knives, and chemicals strewn across the pages of this notorious book. Samantha was adopted when she was only two, and she had five siblings who were biological children of her adopted parents. Samantha even tried to strangle her infant sibling just because she was curious to see what would happen. In this case, could it really be nurtured? Samantha's psychopathic traits were already strongly designed in her genetic code.

Children of this nature will be institutionalized after repeated violent offenses within their families. However, not every psychopath burned kitten tails and drowned puppies as a child. Whether psychopathy is nature or nurture is a gray area that can't be indefinitely proven yet. How a psychopath becomes who they are might be a bit of both, and it's something science still needs to establish for certain, but there's one thing we can know about psychopaths. We know how they operate, so we can recognize their traits.

Identifiable Traits

Thank goodness there's only one percent of severe psychopaths globally, but that doesn't mean milder psychopaths and sociopaths don't exist. An antisocial personality disorder is interchangeably referred to as either sociopathic or psychopathic, but some differences remain. The two disorders show similar traits though. Both types of ASPD people are relentless in pursuing their agenda. They seek power and personal gain without considering morals. Research suggests higher percentages of milder psychopathy among the world's population (Ni, 2018). It's estimated that four percent of the world's population is sociopathic, and mild psychopathic tendencies exist among five to fifteen percent of the population. Mild psychopathy is considered as almost being psychopathic, but not quite. However, psychopathic traits of any magnitude are identifiable.

A psychopath doesn't care for morality, rules, or laws. Most people can distinguish wrongs from rights. You know that it's wrong to drive over the speed limit, steal something from a store, or abuse someone. Cheating, cruelty, and violently attacking someone in the streets are wrong. Being kind, honest, compassionate, and hard-working is morally correct. Obeying the laws of your local society is also correct. However, psychopaths are inclined to break every rule and moral they can. They often have brushes with the law or their relationships deteriorate because they're abusive. A psychopath sees morality as a weakness, and they'll only consider a pretentious 'fairness' if they can gain something from it. They might even use false morality to serve their agenda.

Psychopaths also appear callous, cold-hearted, or emotionless toward the pain and suffering they bring upon others. They don't understand or share empathy with people, even if they caused their suffering. They lack the ability to reflect on their actions and consequences, and they can be categorized as having no humanity, which is a dangerous stew for anyone who stands between them and what they desire. A lack of humanity means they'll repeat transgressions against others, and they'll abuse someone without a second thought. They also don't learn from their transgressions. They won't even consider the suffering their actions could bring to someone else if they paused to think about it. Moreover, they'll make you feel like the transgressor by manipulating you to think they were your victim.

Turning the tables on their victims, a psychopath can also commonly use gaslighting. Gaslighting is a gradual but persistent brainwashing technique that may make their victims doubt their own actions. For example, *I would say that you caused my behavior by not giving me enough attention. It's your fault that I sought attention from another woman because I can't stand your neglect. You only have yourself to blame.* This is gaslighting if I were a psychopath turning the tables on my wife. Gaslighting is any form of psychological bullying that makes the other person question their identity, self-esteem, beliefs, and even reality. People who belittle or undermine others consistently are gaslighting. It's a subtle but powerful manipulation that makes you reconsider your adequacy and desirability.

Psychopaths will rather become the victim than show remorse for their actions, even if you catch them in the act. They're likely to amplify their aggressiveness and defensiveness when challenged. They'll become hostile, deny their responsibility, and blame others for their actions. Most psychopaths create a victim story they can easily fall back on when the heat rises. Their victim mentality is just a way to justify their immoral actions but don't be fooled. The investment guru caught for money laundering will come with all sorts of stories about how he was set up. The husband who beats his wife will tell the police about how she mentally abuses him and the children. The businessman who cuts salaries and overworks his staff will cry victimhood because everyone does it. A psychopath always has a sad, soppy story to defend themselves. They're quick thinkers.

Psychopaths are also pathological liars who don't even care if you find out the truth. Their ability to lie exceeds what you may notice. Psychopaths will lie to progress their agendas, and they'll break promises. What makes this manipulation more dangerous is that they repeat the same lie until it becomes believable. They'll also become quite aggressive if you challenge their lie that isn't even factual. For example, a psychopath keeps telling his friends that his wife sleeps around. He hasn't been spending much time with his friends, and he'd love to have more opportunities to manipulate them, so he makes it look like his wife's cheating. This carries on for two years before his wife divorces him, and now, his friends can write character statements about how his wife made his life hell. So, the psychopath walks away unscathed while his wife has nothing to her name. Sadly, the lies they tell are normally far from the truth, but they don't care if you know that.

Psychopaths are also synonymously famous for being the bully among your friends, colleagues, or relatives. A psychopath's perfect victim is a soft person who doesn't fight back or someone they envy. They have a narcissistic tendency to feel superior to anyone else, and people who make them feel inferior are their targets.

Perhaps someone receives a promotion at work before the psychopath, and this makes them jealous. They believe in all their might that they were better for the job. They have a sense of entitlement. In this case, the psychopath may undermine their colleague by spreading rumors and lies at work to manipulate their employer to see their victim in a different light. This superiority complex also gives them the green light to bully soft people because they believe the reluctance to fight back is confirmation of their superiority.

Three more traits are common among psychopaths. They also get bored easily, so they're always seeking a thrill, often at the expense of others. They may pass snide remarks to upset people on purpose because they're addicted to the thrill that follows stress. Their reckless trait also shines in a way that makes them seem all over the place. They're always trying elaborate stunts and not caring about who gets hurt in their wake. For example, a psychopath might invest all their life's savings in a failing company without discussing it with their spouse. When everything is lost, they'll take no responsibility for their risky behaviors. Finally, psychopaths are also excessively charming, but it's superficial, so watch out. Overly charming traits can be a sign of manipulation. Psychopaths could make you fall in love with their ideas and speeches to subtly encourage you to do things their way.

Every trait can be mild or severe, so don't think someone who manipulates your relationship once in a while to address their agenda is simply passionate about what they want. On the other hand, not every charming person is a psychopath. Psychopaths normally possess multiple selfish traits. Nonetheless, you know what a general psychopath may look like now.

Chapter 2:

Inside the Brain of a Psychopath

Exploring the psychopathic mind allows you to discover the reasons behind what makes them behave the way they do. Their minds and brains don't function the same way as regular people's minds do. A psychopath's mind is not ordinarily one you can fully understand, but that's why researchers are expanding their work to see if we can achieve a better comprehension for treatments and to reduce violence. The main focus is to comprehend how a psychopath thinks and behaves and how their habits manifest in the brain.

The Mind of a Psychopath

Psychopaths have likely been among us for as long as humans existed, but it was the likes of widely-known Herman Mudgett in the 19th century who made waves as America's first serial killer that ignited questions about how some people think the way they do. People couldn't understand how someone could take the life of another human. It's happened countless times in history, but premeditatedly taking a person's life wasn't part of a world war or a crime of passion. It was a brutal and unexplainable occurrence. Questions must be asked whenever someone behaves in a way that doesn't consider someone else's human rights. And this is truer when the killer repeats his crimes. It's hair-raising to think that one in every 100 people are cold-blooded chameleons hiding among us.

Psychopathy became a name we give to blood-thirsty predators who lack remorse, empathy, and impulse control. This is where a name synonymous with the work and research surrounding serial killers comes to light. Psychologist Robert Hare embraced the curiosity that led him to start unraveling a psychopath's mind (Egan, 2016). Hare accidentally stumbled into psychopathy when he had his master's degree in psychology from the University of Alberta. His initial curiosity was about what drives human emotion, motivation, and perception. Hare was enlisted at the British Columbia Penitentiary in 1960, and this is where his first encounter with a true psychopath happened. It's frightening to think that only 20 percent of psychopathy researchers have ever met a psychopath, but Hare was one of the lucky ones who did if you can call it that.

Within Hare's first hour at the penitentiary, he encountered a man who made him doubt his job. He calls the man 'Ray,' and this guy pulled out a handmade knife to threaten Hare. Somehow, Hare chose to swallow his fear and continue his chat with Ray, who then saw Hare wasn't a pushover, so he started threatening to kill his cellmate. Hare took many risks by not pushing the panic button or reporting Ray to the guards for his threats about his cellmate, but Ray never followed through. Ray became a charming and civilized person over the 10 months Hare worked at the penitentiary, and Hare even recommended him to work in the auto shop. Hare thought he got through to this man, and he was surprised to find that his car's brakes were tampered with when he left to pursue an academic position. Fortunately, Hare survived, but he understood that Ray's charm was superficial.

This didn't deter Hare. Instead, he returned to the penitentiary later to work with the prisoners because that's where the majority of psychopaths were. With the help of the Bronx Veterans Affairs Medical Center, Hare conducted the first-ever brain scans on psychopaths within prison populations in 1991. The participants had to look at neutral and emotional words like table, desk, maggot, and corpse while hooked up to an electroencephalogram (EEG). Regular people show an emotional surge when they look at pictures of words like corpse and torture. It naturally creates a response that can be seen on the EEG. However, psychopaths showed no emotional surge while reading the worst of words.

Neuroimaging is now being integrated into many courtrooms, and it even helped in the trial against Brian Dugan, earning him the death penalty in 2009. Hare is among a few experts who believe that neuroimaging in the courtroom could become as common as deoxyribonucleic acid (DNA) evidence. The biggest challenge in psychopathy remains the fact that experts can't agree on where it originates. Some experts believe nurture is the origin, especially with abuse and trauma, but others believe the structural differences in the brain are to blame for psychopathy. This disorder has major implications on the world, and Hare believes that specialized treatments and therapies are necessary for adult and child psychopaths. A psychopath could lead a somewhat normal life if the treatments are designed according to the variances found in the psychopathic brain versus regular ones.

Hare is famously known for his development of the Psychopathy Checklist-Revised (PCL-R) test. His test measures a collection of 20 personality behaviors and traits, which either indicate a lack of psychopathy or an abundance of it. The Hare test is the number one violence risk assessment tool in North America, and it's commonly used by forensic psychologists. His test makes its way into the courtroom for the most dangerous and high-risk prisoners post-sentencing and during parole hearings. The average person who has no psychopathic traits or behaviors will score below five, but severe psychopaths will score between 30 and 40.

The Hidden Suffering of Psychopaths

It's strange to use those words in the same sentence, but psychopaths also have suffering, whether they turn this into their victimhood or not. A psychopath is defined as someone who lacks judgment, has superficial charm, is highly intelligent, but doesn't learn from their actions. Believe it or not, many psychopaths care deeply about their families, children, and even pets, although they do so in their own way. A psychopath struggles to love and trust the rest of humanity. They also exude this superiority complex, but little do many people know that they feel inferior to others. They're also mostly aware of how their behavior stigmatizes them. Psychopaths are the kind of people who aim higher than most, and they believe they can do more than the people they compare themselves to, but they often suffer from a lack of gratification when things don't go their way.

Unrealistic expectations and community or relative conflicts can lead their risky adventures straight into disappointment. Suffering can be the inability to meet your expectations if you set them too high, and psychopaths are risk-takers by nature. Some psychopaths are also discouraged by their lack of success or desired outcomes. They're always in pursuit of a great outcome, but that doesn't happen for many of them. A psychopath wants to be perfect at everything they do, even when they hurt someone. Disappointment is abundant, and that can discourage anyone's mental well-being. Psychopaths lack the type of fear regular people have to stop themselves from taking risks. Their associated lack of being able to learn from their mistakes doesn't make it easier. Instead, they end up in confrontations with themselves and others.

Violent psychopaths reach the edge of no return. This happens when they feel like they've tried everything and bolstered every connection, but still, they failed. At this point, they feel disconnected from the world, and this is where it gets dangerous. A psychopath's ability to value someone's life declines, and they might even see their own lives as worthless. People don't realize that loneliness, a great sense of failure, and an inferiority complex this large can lead to a violent psychopath. Suddenly, the risk of aggression towards people increases, and they're just as likely to be aggressive toward themselves. What makes a psychopath suffer even more is that treatment is so limited, even if they wanted to lead normal lives. The stigma around psychopathy makes them question whether they should seek treatment, and the treatments don't all work for every psychopath.

Some violent types of psychopathy are untreatable at this stage. Even long-term psychotherapy won't help some psychopaths. Understandably, psychopaths can become disheartened and give in to their urges. All hope is not lost for most psychopaths though. A combination of neurofeedback, psychotherapy, and psychopharmacology could be the answer. Neurofeedback is when brain scans are used to show a psychopath how their brain functions, and they're taught to gradually change these functions, which are then seen with their own eyes. According to research published by psychiatrist Willem Martens (2014), targeting the traits within a psychopath's brain could provide better treatment. Emotional pain, social isolation, hidden suffering, and a lack of self-esteem are why psychopaths are potentially turning violent, so it could be fruitful to diminish the factors that cause psychopaths to act up.

Chemical changes in the brain are responsible for some of the reinforcement of traits. Sensation-seeking traits may indicate that a psychopath has a lack of cortisol arousal. Cortisol is the stress hormone, and it's accompanied by adrenaline, which both offer gratification for the pursuit of sensations. The same trait has been shown to accompany a high level of testosterone and a low level of monoamine oxidase (MAO). Low levels of serotonin in psychopaths have also been noted in Martens's work. Serotonin is the regulator of many other hormones, and other imbalances were noted that could also explain the lack of proper function in the hypothalamus-pituitary-adrenal, or HPA, axis. This part of the brain is closely related to how people respond to stimuli, and improper function could partly explain a lack of emotional responses.

If you consider the dynamics of changing biochemical treatments in medication to complement psychotherapy and neurofeedback, the treatment of psychopathy could change. Reducing impulsivity, emotional suffering, and aggression in psychopaths could be promising.

Psychopaths and addicts have commonalities, and approaching their treatments with a multi-faceted method could change the way psychopaths live, but it can also become addictive. Psychopaths have a higher risk of abusing substances, especially when they're not receiving the appropriate care for their emotional suffering. Their loneliness and sense of failure can make them turn to drugs and alcohol. It can also cause addictive tendencies to prescription medication. Therefore, the treatments would have to be guided by strict policies, which aren't always accepted by psychopaths.

Fortunately, the American Medical Association (AMA) under the Biden administration is changing the priorities for drug treatments in America (Kuntz, 2021). To treat psychopaths with medication without feeding an addictive personality requires seven priorities. Access to treatment must expand, advancement of racial equality is required, and increasing the research to reduce any potential harms is a priority. Proven efforts to reduce the susceptibility of addiction are also a priority, and so is controlling the supply of illicit substances to prevent the abuse thereof. Other priorities are to establish workplace recovery awareness and supportive services to supplement medicinal treatments. Funding has been allocated to ensure all seven priorities are addressed appropriately. AMA completely supports drug-based treatments under these conditions.

The progress of their lives and a lack of support for psychopaths also encourage their suffering, which only turns them into severe psychopaths if we don't do something about it. A psychopath's lack of civilized mentality is also to blame on chemicals in the brain. However, their brains also look different, and their personality traits could be challenging to overcome.

What Drives Their Selfishness?

Psychopaths are extremely selfish, but that doesn't change the fact that one percent of non-institutionalized American men are psychopathic (Sandoiu & Collier, 2018). Psychopaths are 20 to 25 times more likely to be incarcerated for crimes than other people, and 50 percent of violent crimes are committed by psychopaths in America. A lack of empathy is a trademark trait of psychopaths, and it could explain some of their selfishness. Being unable to empathize with another person's needs automatically leads to self-centeredness. Psychopaths don't have the neurological ability to empathize.

A study published in *Frontiers in Human Neuroscience* focused on the lack of empathy in psychopaths (Decety et al., 2013). The study included scanning the brains of 121 prisoners during two phases. They were shown images of painful situations and asked to imagine how this feels if it happened to them, and their brains lit up in various regions. The anterior insula, right amygdala, and somatosensory cortex activated when they had to empathize with their own pain. However, the prisoners were then asked to imagine this same situation inflicting pain on someone else, and the results were undeniable in the favor of them not having empathy toward others. The same brain regions remained dormant in the second phase, proving that empathy for others was not neurologically activated. The psychopaths were measured on Hare's scale first, so the high-functioning psychopaths were intelligent and capable of other normal brain functions.

Psychopaths struggle with impulsivity as well, so that could further increase their selfishness because they don't consider broader options before making a decision. The broader options include other people. Some people have even claimed that psychopaths aren't necessarily evil. They think psychopaths are incapable of making decisions without impulsivity. Harvard University studied impulsivity in 49 prisoners to see if they really struggled to make decisions (Hosking et al., 2017). Brain scans were used to determine what happens in the prefrontal cortex during delayed gratification exercises. The prisoners were given an option to receive less money immediately or wait for a larger amount. An area called the ventral striatum in the prefrontal cortex is known to activate when we anticipate rewards, and severe psychopaths showed abundant activation, more so than can be expected in a regular person who will wait for delayed rewards.

The ventral striatum can place too much value on immediate gratification, which doesn't allow psychopaths to consider how much better things could be tomorrow. If they were offered a million dollars to kill someone, but they had to do it now, they would do it, according to the Harvard study. Impulsivity is a dangerous way to make decisions. What these studies also prove is that psychopathy expresses faulty brain circuits. That's one thing on which most scientists and psychologists can agree. The question that stands in the way of understanding why psychopathic brains look different is what causes the differences. A study by Radboud University in the Netherlands may shed some light on the connection between brain malfunctions and psychopathy (Volman et al., 2016). The study included 15 psychopathic prisoners and compared them to 19 regular people as a control group.

The prisoners showed a strong disconnection between the amygdala and the prefrontal cortex compared to the control group, but what stood out even more than the structural differences was that the psychopaths had an abnormal amount of testosterone in the prefrontal cortex. The prefrontal cortex is designed to help a regular person judge emotion and make decisions about how they should respond to someone. The disconnection between the emotional amygdala and the prefrontal cortex already made this challenging for psychopaths, but testosterone enhances the challenge. It also explains why 75 percent of psychopaths are men. They naturally produce more testosterone, which can inhibit the activity in the prefrontal cortex, meaning that psychopaths have two factors working against them. They must reestablish a connection between the two regions, and they must control their testosterone levels.

What the Netherlands study proved again though is that a biochemical or hormonal influence may also be present in psychopaths, which means it can be treated to some extent. Even the brain can be treated and changed because it's plastic. New synapses or connections can be forged between different brain regions with persistent effort. That's what makes a combination of medication, psychotherapy, and neurofeedback so valuable. Watching progressive changes in the brain can start releasing chemicals that could reinforce the new connections. The greatest challenge in neuroplasticity is that psychopaths don't feel remorse or regret. Positive reinforcement might be more useful than trying to punish them to change their behaviors. Violent behaviors aren't condoned by humanity, and punishment will always be preferred above retribution.

Nevertheless, the brain helps us understand that a psychopath isn't always decisively selfish. It's the way their brains work that makes them narcissistic.

Clues You're Dealing With a Psychopath

The term psychopath is often used to refer to less dangerous people, too. However, people with less dangerous traits were once considered sociopaths. Modern research has made clearer distinctions between milder and more severe psychopaths (Hirstein, 2017). Psychopaths who have their genes and innate traits to blame are often referred to as primary psychopaths. Those who have their environment to blame more than their genes are called secondary psychopaths. Primary psychopaths are the more dangerous kind who commonly become violent. Psychopaths are categorized through one of three systems that measure their criteria. The psychopathy checklist revised is one method, and some psychoanalysts use the psychopathic personality inventory (PPI).

Another method commonly used is the diagnostic and statistical manual of mental disorders (DSM). The DSM and the PCL-R refer to psychopathic personality disorders as an antisocial personality disorder, and the PCL-R is the most commonly used list to determine whether someone is psychopathic and how severe it is based on the listed criteria. Two of the criteria for this list can help you identify a psychopath. The first clue is that the person will be undeterred by disgust, and the second clue is that they won't respond to emotional cues. Psychologist Abigail Marsh from Georgetown University has conducted various studies relating to the ability of psychopaths to perceive fear in others (Bering, 2009). Not only do psychopaths lack fear themselves, but they also can't see it in others.

Marsh found that psychopaths can't detect fear among other emotions. A psychopath is unable to correctly process the emotional cues they see in other people's faces. Without being able to process it, they can't respond to it. Fear is displayed as a social cue or distress call to encourage another person to stop what they're doing. Our faces give signals to another person's brain, but a psychopath's brain works differently. The information is fine in top-down processing, meaning the psychopath sees the cues. Their brains aren't blind to facial and verbal cues. However, the bottom-up processing that sends the information to the prefrontal cortex to decipher a decision or response is missing. This isn't always seen in severe psychopaths alone.

Let's say you're worried about an exam tomorrow, and your friend shows no consideration for your feelings. A friend who shows consideration or supportive feedback can process your facial and verbal cues correctly. A friend who continues to convince you to leave your studies and join them for a party may be showing mild psychopathy. Take another example where your boss asks you to work overtime tonight, even though you have to be alone in the office until midnight, and the crime in your area is rising exponentially. In a sense, your boss is inflicting fear or pain on you, and their inability to understand how you feel might be a sign that they're mildly psychopathic. A persistently inconsiderate person is potentially a clue that you're dealing with a psychopath, even if they're not the violent kind. A psychopath's aggression toward a victim would continue, irrespective of their fear and screams because they can't use bottom-up processing to respond appropriately.

Psychopaths are also shallow and void of guilt, according to the PCL-R criteria. They show little to no emotions, including guilt, shame, and fear. They won't be afraid of pain and the anticipation of it as easily as a normal person. Not only will their brains not activate the same way regular people's brains do, but they also won't show common signs of fear like sweating or skin color changes. Psychopaths don't normally have fears. They won't be terrified of heights or spiders. They'll face a bear in the woods and think they'll win. Whatever emotions they do show will be subtle or shallow. Disgust is another crucial factor in the criteria, and it can offer the second clue. A lack of disgust is just another way psychopaths are immune to emotional responses. What is your reaction when you see a dead body in a movie or roadkill on your journey?

Regular people have a response to disgusting images and words. The disconnected regions that control emotion and judgment are somewhat responsible for the lack of disgust. Psychopaths can't feel emotions as deeply as a normal person, so they don't easily process information as disgusting. Regular people are normally disgusted by things that don't fit societal norms. They're disgusted by a rat running across the floor or someone stealing something from their store. Disgust is an ethical challenge, and psychopaths have no ethical morals. A clue you're dealing with a psychopath is when someone has no understandable reaction to a photo of mutilated bodies or even a foul odor. Odors also require processing because all the five senses are collecting top-down data. It's the bottom-up processing that doesn't work, so foul odors might not even be noticed.

Unraveling the psychopathic brain is technical, but it makes sense once you understand what science has proven so far. Clues can help you stay safe among the potential predators lurking about. They can also help you identify psychopathy in yourself. However, knowing what a psychopath may look like in all the people closest to you can certainly save your health, happiness, success, and maybe your life.

Chapter 3:

Psychopaths Around You

We all know someone odd or manipulative to some degree. Perhaps you have a friend who seems unusually self-centered or a partner who always gets their way. Maybe your boss expects the unexpected from you, or your child has a strange and worrying nature. Whether your mind wanders off to the aunt who happily turns every family gathering into a brawl or your brother grew up as the local bully, chances are that you know a psychopath. You may even be one yourself. You need to know what psychopaths look like to manage your interactions with them.

Recognizing a Psychopath

Recognizing a psychopath isn't always easy. You'll know that a psychopath can appear as an awkward but sweet young boy if you watched *The Bates Motel*. You'll realize how charming and intelligent a psychopath can appear if you watched *Hannibal*. Psychopaths are everywhere, and the extent of their psychopathy is unknown unless they've been tested. However, there are tell-tale signs that you're dealing with a psychopath.

The extent of their manipulative nature is beyond what normal people express. Sometimes, the manipulation is as subtle as a friend who makes you feel bad so you do what they desire. You want to stay home, but they want to go clubbing. They'll feed your emotions until you give up. Other times, the manipulation is outright.

A psychopath is also skilled at reading people quickly. They do this as a means to manipulate you. They find your weaknesses to exploit them. This is obvious in the new dating trend called negging, which is when a psychopath uses your weaknesses to make themselves look better while you feel worse. Anyone who sizes you up in seconds and uses your insecurities against you is potentially a psychopath. They'll collect information from you in close relationships and use it against you when it suits them. Psychopaths hurt people, and what worsens it is that the victims often don't suspect it. Families, friends, and partners are often torn and disgusted by their psychopathic loved one's behavior. Psychopaths will always tell you what you wish to hear. They can be quite dexterous in intimate relationships by confirming what you say just to play with your feelings.

A psychopath will tell their partner to change careers if that's what they want to hear, irrespective of whether it's a rational decision. Sadly, the downright charming nature of psychopaths makes the victim quite ignorant of their oppressors' true intentions. Psychopaths remain self-centered. They might validate your beliefs so they can exploit them later. It's all within their gain. What they can gain from, they will. A psychopath has no conscience, so they'll behave in a way that makes you question their choices. Moreover, they won't be remorseful when things go wrong. Hearing an apology from a psychopath is rare. A psychopath's life, career, relationships, and goals won't be consistent because they don't fear change like we do. Indeed, a psychopath can love their family and tenaciously pursue goals, but most psychopaths don't stick long with anything.

They'll change jobs often, and they won't have a valid reason for doing so. They'll find it hard to build concrete relationships with their loved ones, albeit they do care for them. Moreover, they'll keep taking risks other people fear, and these risks will sometimes come back to bite everyone involved. Financial and career risks are common among psychopaths. These people have two physical tell-tale signs that something isn't working right in their minds. Their voices are normally monotonous. They don't have many tonalities because they don't feel emotions like we do. The second physical sign is their eyes. A psychopath's eyes are normally dark, unemotional, dead, and lifeless.

You can see emotions in someone's eyes, but psychopaths show none. Our body language is part of our tonality. They can appear charming beyond your dreams, but they may look and sound cold. The simplest way to see how emotionless their tonality is can be by observing them after they've done something questionable. If your friend shows no body language or change of voice after committing an offense against someone else's rights, then you may be dealing with a psychopath. A psychopath wants to control and dominate other people. Their fearless dominance can be seen when they persistently look for your vulnerabilities and weaknesses to use them against you. Psychopaths don't follow the rules. They're adept at lying to your face, and they love telling elaborate tales that attract their victims. Do you know anyone who can lie to your face without blinking?

What makes it worse is that their lies seem believable, and they don't care who gets hurt in their pursuit to gain something. In business, a psychopath makes excuses, saying that their lies are profitable for everyone. Sociopaths learn this behavior, but psychopaths are born like this. The more weaknesses a victim has, the more likely the psychopath is to take advantage of them. Unfortunately, we can't test everyone on Hare's PCL-R test unless they want it or they're caught committing a crime. The test is great to assess the severity of psychopathy, but it's not possible to ask every friend if we can assess them. This may actually turn them aggressive because they'll realize you're on to them.

Robert Hare spent decades studying prisoners and people with mental disorders who also breached the rights of other humans. Our understanding of the psychopath's brain may still be in its early days, but exactly how mental disorders reinforce personality defects is still unclear. Psychopathy is generally an undesirable way of being. If your gut tells you that someone is odd, you might have to listen closer. The purest of psychopaths would probably score 40 on the PCL-R, but anyone who scores above 30 is diagnosable as a psychopath. Most people who haven't engaged in criminal activities would probably score around five on the PCL-R. However, some people might score a little higher, which isn't always bad news. In some situations, having a few psychopathic traits could be an advantage in the pursuit of greatness. Some corporate faces are where they are today because of their determined fortitude.

Someone who uses their lack of fear to push themselves to the top of their industry without crushing people's rights can be a mild psychopath. Remember that they're not all violent, and some of them can even teach you how to pursue greater career positions. The problem with psychopaths is that they know what you're feeling, but they can't comprehend it on the same terms. They don't feel the emotions you do. Their lack of empathy can be advantageous in business because they lack emotional reasoning. They can see their goals and ambitions with logic, which isn't always possible when we're driven by emotions. They understand their thoughts because they don't have emotions clouding their judgments. This is bad when it comes to violent psychopaths, but career-driven psychopaths can reach the top of the ladder before others.

Psychopaths also believe they're more logical than other people, which might increase their motivation. Some psychopaths don't even realize what they are because of their ability to rationalize. This makes it more challenging to recognize one who isn't violent or outright psychopathic. James Fallon from the University of California is one example of someone who seems so rational and normal that he never recognized his own traits (Bold, 2019). Fallon is a well-known neuroscientist who researches the minds of serial killers. He's often on *Criminal Minds*. After he spoke about his research that led to identifying 30 psychopaths among 70 people in a double-blind study, Fallon received an interesting call from his mother. His mom asked him if he thought he came from a normal family, and to Fallon's surprise, he didn't. He was related to infamous killer Lizzie Borden, who axed her stepfather and mother in Massachusetts in 1892.

Fallon wanted to know if anyone in his living family was genetically predisposed to psychopathy. He compared eight of his relatives' brain scans and genetic sequencing to that of serial killers, and his results were what he called embarrassing. Fallon found out that he was a psychopath. He found five genes that correlate with psychopathy, and his orbital cortex was inactive. The orbital cortex is related to ethics, morals, impulsivity, and aggression. However, Fallon explains that his nurture trumped his nature. He grew up in a loving home, and his genetic and underlying brain malfunctions were never reinforced by early childhood abuse or trauma. Fallon believes that it's hard to classify all psychopaths as violent or dangerous, especially if they've used these traits to pursue greater success in life.

This predicament makes it difficult to call psychopathy a mental disorder, but it is one. Psychopathy is unlike other mental disorders because it feels more 'pleasant.' Imagine not being restricted by emotional influence when you're thinking, acting, or pursuing goals.

Anyway, the various psychopath tools and tests can help identify antisocial personality disorder, but it's not always an option if you can't convince your loved ones to do it. Being able to convince someone to assess themselves can help them receive treatment. At the least, it can help the family learn about the disorder. Talk therapy or even talking to the family of the victims can also help a mild psychopath. However, severe psychopathy or those who have high levels of self-centeredness are unlikely to benefit from treatments. Recognizing a psychopath or understanding yourself as one is the first step to making a difference either way.

Relative Impact

The brunt of having a psychopath in the family influences everyone's lives. In this case, we're referring to psychopaths who have both a personality trait malfunction and a history of criminal activity or antisocial behavior that hurt other people. According to peer-reviewed research published in *Psychopathy – New Updates on an Old Phenomenon*, a few factors of severe psychopathy and family life are important to understand (Leedom, 2017). Psychopaths are considered to be antisocial in the classical sense. Theory suggests that they're unlikely to form long-lasting bonds with other people. However, this isn't entirely accurate. Psychopaths can form lasting bonds with romantic partners, friends, colleagues, siblings, parents, and their children. These relationships aren't normally functional or healthy though.

The review didn't include the rate of victimization between psychopaths and their friends or relatives, but suspicions are rife that these relationships aren't healthy. The risk of these relationships is likely based on the severity of the psychopathic disorder. The more severe the symptoms become, the higher the potential rate of relative and friend victimization rises. One area of the review covered the risks of continued psychopathic tendencies in families if familial relationships are dysfunctional. Problem- or high-risk children who continue to have dysfunctional relationships with their parents in early childhood are more likely to develop severe psychopathy. It's not just the parental relationships that matter, either.

Most American children have at least one sibling, and sibling rivalry or bullying is common. Unfortunately, this can lead to further development of psychopathic tendencies. The rate isn't well-known between sibling abuse and psychopathy, but children can enhance their traits while being a victim or perpetrator. The bully is exercising their psychopathic tendencies, and the victim is being exposed to abuse. Either way, being a bully or a victim enhances the risks. Children also show coercive natures before they become adult psychopaths. They might be the coercer, or their siblings or parents could have this nature. To coerce someone is to convince them to do something they wouldn't normally do. One sibling might coerce another to be cruel to animals.

Parents may coerce children to do unthinkable things like sexual favors.

Coercion and manipulation are very similar, and it's a trait learned in childhood. A child can also be manipulative by demanding things from their parents while playing on their emotions. Currently, the best treatment for this young manipulative nature is by teaching parents how to coach their children to stop being negative and manipulative. Parents must break this cycle in themselves, and ensure that a sibling isn't doing it to their brother or sister. Parenting is a modest factor in the development of psychopathy when children already have the genetic predisposition, but it remains a factor. If you're a parent, you should be assessing yourself and your partner to establish the impact you might have on your children. The review also connected negligent parenting to the development of psychopathy in children.

If you suspect that your partner is a psychopath, and you're not doing anything about it, you're just as responsible for your child's outcome. An evaluation will include four factors if a professional suspects psychopathic traits in a mother or father. The first factor is whether either parent has a grandiose sense of self and expresses themselves manipulatively or charmingly. The second factor is whether they're impulsive, parasitic, and irresponsible. The third factor is whether they lack acceptance, remorse, and empathy. The final factor is whether parents have a history of criminal, delinquent, or antisocial behavior. The presence of anxiety, substance abuse, or mood disorders also indicates risk factors for the children. The four facets and the risk factors could determine whether a child becomes psychopathic.

The review also looked at the correlation between intimate partners and psychopathy. Undoubtedly, severe psychopathy has abysmal consequences on an intimate relationship. The review confirms that psychopaths can be highly abusive toward their partners. Psychopathic tendencies can reduce the relationship satisfaction for both partners, whether you're dating or cohabiting. Primary psychopaths are those who were born that way, but they tend to do better with romantic relationships. It's the psychopaths who were raised to be who they are today that struggle more in intimate relationships. A psychopath's suffering is also further enhanced by their inability to have meaningful and healthy relationships with their partners. This affects a psychopath's mental well-being because they can't feel your emotions, but they can feel their own.

The extent of violence between partners caused by psychopathy isn't well-established. It's considered to be dimensionally responsible for partner-on-partner violence, but it's unknown to which extent. The abuse from a psychopath in an intimate relationship could externalize itself in many forms. Mental, emotional, and physical abuse are but three kinds a victim can endure. They can also experience financial, sexual, social, and legal exploitation. Exploiting your partner's financial health for selfish reasons is a sign of psychopathy. There's a strong association between relationship distress and psychopathy. Many couples in couples therapy are likely there because one or both of them have psychopathic traits (Leedom, 2017).

Everyone in your family and social circle has some kind of influence on your mental health and psychopathic development if you have a genetic predisposition. Whether you're a psychopath or a relative shows signs, something has to be done about it. This is why it's imperative to recognize a psychopath in your circle.

Investigating Closer Relationships

Thanks to the fearlessness and arrogance of most psychopaths, you're able to recognize them through their behaviors and traits. Your best friend could be psychopathic, or you might be the one hurting others, so knowing what to look out for can change the direction of your relationships and life.

Friendly Suspects

Psychopaths are humans, even though they lack humanity and empathy. Some of them can function better than most people, but their underlying personality dysfunctions can make them challenging to be friends with. Their greatest ambition is to see what they can get from you versus how much it will cost them. Most friends have a give-and-take relationship, but psychopaths will take, take, and take some more. They don't like spending energy on the relationship. Under the right circumstances, a psychopathic friend will offer an unexpected blow at the worst time, and they won't think twice about it. They're fundamentally evil, and they have a greater capacity for being malicious and cruel than most people.

Psychopaths obsess over the dark triad, which is commonly glorified among people who spend much of their time in the manosphere. The manosphere is an online community that opposes feminism. However, the dark triad is a personality pyramid used in psychology. Everyone has a little narcissism in them, but dark triad personality types have a combination of narcissism, psychopathy, and Machiavellianism, which is the pursuit of power. Machiavellianism is when someone sees the world as a power struggle, so they'll wait and pounce when the time is right. Psychopathic friends are highly decisive in ethically ambiguous scenarios, but this often costs them friends. "Nice guys" are often the imitation of this superhuman who supposedly sympathizes with you and befriends you until they have what they need and then exploit you.

Some psychopathic friends can also be sadistic. For example, one of your friends might see it as a natural challenge to overpower you or another friend by banging your girlfriend. They just want to show you that they can do it. They want to show dominance. Any friend who appears to compete with you or to make decisions without acknowledging the impact it has on you might be psychopathic. Psychopathic friends also express more judgment than necessary. Ironically, those who judge others are often hypocrites. The act of pointing fingers at someone else only removes the spotlight from them. A friend who takes no responsibility for their actions is likely psychopathic. Low-intelligence psychopaths won't easily be as judgmental as high-intelligence psychopaths. A low-intelligence psychopath will likely only spin the blame bottle once they're cornered, but then they'll go full throttle.

High-intelligence psychopaths play a camouflage game. Their judgment will be directed subtly because they don't want other intelligent people to recognize their lies. They'll direct the blame for issues with such believable and elaborate lies that you might not notice at first that they're redirecting the guilt to others. This is called misdirection. A psychopathic friend will pretend to speak from a moral viewpoint when judging someone else's behavior, but this is only smoke and mirrors. A friend might tell you a story about how their partner deliberately tore old family photos apart, but they don't tell you about the ex-girlfriend to whom they always compare their partner. They direct judgment to their partner for their behavior, but they don't shine a light on their provocative actions.

Ask yourself if a friend has acted without hesitation before doing something immoral, especially when they were drunk. Alcohol has a way of showing us people's true natures. Consider whether a friend thinks mechanically about social encounters or opportunities. Mechanical thinking and over-obsessing might be signs that emotions aren't part of the decision-making process. People who are too aware of their actions are either intelligent empaths or psychopaths. Psychopaths will use misdirection to blame others for their shortfalls, and they'll be highly ambitious because they don't have empathy. They'll also be charming enough to seem like the light of every party. Be wary of these people.

There's one rule with psychopathic friends. It's time to cut them off unless you know what they want from you. Know that they want something because everything is about them and their progress. There's nothing to be gained from having a severe female psychopathic friend, and you should only continue a cautious friendship with male psychopaths if you know there's something you're getting in return. Indeed, you have to think about yourself. Psychopaths can teach you a lot of valuable things fast and efficiently. You can use these lessons of unrelenting desire to positively boost your inner psychopathic traits to reach your goals and achieve greater success. What you need to realize is that psychopaths as teachers will always seek more power. You must embrace them with savage and cunning intentions to survive their power struggle with you.

The winner is the person willing to sacrifice the most. If your friends don't offer learned ambition, then it's time to cut them off. It's for your sanity. Don't be empathetic toward psychopathic friends because they're not empathetic toward you. Get rid of any friends who only gain from you and offer nothing in return. The most you could probably gain from a psychopath is to learn their tenacity.

Parenting a Monster

Every child tends to push your buttons. Naughtiness is not a sign of psychopathy. However, you need to get help for your child if they're showing signs of psychopathy. Animal cruelty is one of the main signs your child will become a psychopath. Many children pull a cat's tail, but they stop when you explain how this hurts the animal because they have empathy. However, worry if your child continues to be cruel to animals by kicking, hurting, or killing them. They may already be a little sadistic and desire continuous cruelty toward animals that can't speak against them.

Consider whether your child is also a pyromaniac. Do they love playing with matches or setting things alight? Pyromania is a way children express aggression and defiance. Enuresis is when a child wets the bed, but it can also lead to signs of psychopathy. Children get embarrassed when they wet the bed, and they may set fires or carry the kitten around by its throat to express their frustration. One reason children who suffer from enuresis are more likely to become psychopathic is that they also get bullied for their embarrassing lack of control. You should watch your child's behavior closely if they wet the bed at six years or older.

Children who constantly violate the rules are also potential psychopaths in the making. Children breaking rules doesn't guarantee psychopathy, especially if they show remorse for their actions. It's also normal if they just feel bad about it. Kids who break rules and find joy in it are concerning. A child who steals from others or bullies another child incessantly is worrisome. Moreover, they'll lie about it when they're caught. They'll redirect the blame to anyone else. They also don't care if you know they're lying. In fact, they'll throw a tantrum at any age just to prove you wrong.

Bullying is a sign of psychopathy in the making, but insensitivity is a subtler warning. Psychopathic children don't feel fear, compassion, or stress the same way other children do, so they might try to coerce other kids to do things that make them uncomfortable. They might touch another child's private parts, or they might take what belongs to another child without caring how that child feels. A psychopathic teenager might cry out for attention when their sibling receives extra attention after experiencing a traumatic event because they're insensitive to their feelings. Any signs of psychopathy in your child should be shared with a professional to nip it in the bud as much as possible.

Dating a Psychopath

The one person you want to know whether they're a psychopath is your partner. Psychopaths are brazen risk-takers who behave antisocially every chance they get, and they seem emotionally resilient because of their impaired empathy and fear. They're mean, impulsive, and arrogant, and they don't feel sorry for what they do to you. This is in their nature, and you're not easily going to change them. They must seek help themselves, or they won't change, so dating a psychopath makes you brave, too. Recognizing a psychopathic partner could change your entire life. The first sign you're dating a psychopath is that they'll lie through their teeth to conceal their interests and goals. And if you catch them lying, they'll turn it around to make you feel guilty, and they'll top it off with some more lies.

A psychopath will continually deceive you for their own benefit. They'll make you doubt your suspicions by turning up their superficial charm that got you hooked in the first place. Pathological lying isn't the only trait they express in romantic relationships. Your partner might study your behavior and use it against you. They know your weaknesses, and they'll exploit whatever they can to make you feel like the bad guy. A few common traits in romantic relationships have been confirmed in psychopaths because it's the way their brains function (Tzani-Pepelasi, 2018). Their level of manipulation might even be similar to a toddler's tantrum when they don't get their way. Nagging or repetitive conversations might be prevalent in the relationship, and they won't consider your feelings when they make decisions.

A psychopath's brain is wired to be more likely to cheat on you. The higher they score on a psychopathy test, the more likely they'll cheat. It's exhausting to be with someone who shows relentless selfishness. Detaching yourself from a psychopath might make them appear to feel sorry, but this is as superficial as their charm. They only feel sorry for themselves because they can't dominate or control you anymore. However, you're unlikely to get a psychopath back once you dump them because they know you're not easy to dominate. Psychopaths are parasites, always sucking on what they can while giving nothing back. They love one-sided romantic relationships. Some people can see past these negative traits and accept their partners for who they are, but you'd still have to recognize them as psychopaths.

Some warning signs that you're dating a psychopath include love bombing, extreme infatuation from day one, amplified flattery, and idealization. Love bombing is when you're overwhelmed by romantic gestures long before you even know each other. Infatuation and true attraction are different, so be careful. Idealization is when they make you think this relationship will be perfect in every way. Perfection is a lie. A psychopath will also gain your sympathy quickly by telling you about their victimhood. They prey on your emotions. They'll also involve you in self-proclaimed and imagined love triangles, such as a married man promising you the world. Men who make women partake in threesomes when she doesn't want to are also psychopathic.

Psychopaths will try to relentlessly change reality, and they'll even make you question your emotions when they provoked them in the first place. You can't dare feel down because that's not what they expect from you, but they're the ones making you feel worthless and unloved. They intentionally provoke you to feel the opposite of what they expect. A psychopath will also intentionally provoke jealousy and rivalry by telling you that your friend inappropriately looks at them. They get kicks from seeing you stew at a friend while they pretend to be innocent. Meanwhile, they're flirting with your friend. Psychopaths also avoid promoting your self-esteem, and they'll withhold attention to make you feel unloved. They have a crippling, selfish need for attention themselves.

When dating a psychopath, you may not recognize your own feelings anymore. You may have more questions than answers, which indicates an unhealthy attachment. Your partner should never make you question your identity, worth, beliefs, or feelings. Now, you know how to spot a vulture in your life, but you also need to know the difference between a sociopath and a psychopath.

Chapter 4:

Psychopath Versus Sociopath

Once you realize how common psychopathy is in the real world, you may start questioning whether people are sociopaths or psychopaths. The names are interchangeably used to describe someone who behaves antisocially, but there are distinct differences. Knowing what differentiates the two types of ASPD can help you understand what may be expected from these people. Their behaviors differ slightly, and it's good to know which psychopathic mind is calculated and which is disorganized. This is how you get ahead of a psychopath and size them up like they do with you. It might also show you which type of psychopath you are if you recognize yourself as one.

Distinguishing Similarities

Psychopathy is not as taboo as you might think. Sure, we all know the cinematic remakes of people like Ted

Bundy and John the Ripper, but many people don't realize that they watch numerous psychopaths on television all the time. You must remember that a psychopath has more than one definition. They're not all killers, even though some modern television programs seem to create these archetypes of villains-turned-heroes. Other subtler versions of psychopaths and possibly sociopaths are commonly depicted in popular shows. Take Oliver Queen from *Arrow* as one example. Everyone sees him as a hero because he returns to fictional Starling City after being tortured for years on an island among other places. Everyone roots for Oliver because he came back from the dead to rid his city of villains and criminals. He wanted to right his father's wrongs.

What people forget to realize with Oliver is that he was turned into a monster who thought he had the right to take the lives of other people. The people who died at his hands are not his to take, irrespective of what crimes they committed. Oliver has no morals, and he doesn't value the lives of the people in his city, even though he pretends to. Thousands of people die because of his father's mistakes, which means Oliver might be both a psychopath and a sociopath. He was born into a family of psychopaths, and his torture conditioned his habits to kill. Bar the fact that he's a hot-headed killer, people love his archetype on the show. Anyway, Oliver is an easy-to-spot sociopath just like Dexter. However, a psychopath who isn't easy to distinguish is Sheldon Cooper from *The Big Bang Theory*.

Sheldon struggles with his emotions, and his number one goal is to control his friends at any cost. Sheldon might be more of a sociopath than a psychopath, albeit he never truly had a bad childhood. His high-level intelligence could make him calculative, but his inability to respond appropriately to his friends could lean toward a sociopath. Sheldon is like a child who will throw the biggest tantrum to get his way, and underneath it all, he doesn't understand how he hurts his friends. I think it's safe to say that Sheldon is a combination of sociopath and psychopath. The bottom line is that we watch these programs without realizing the mentality of the main characters. Sure, these shows are entertaining, but it's almost as though psychopathy is becoming normalized in society now, or at least, within the fictional world.

Nonetheless, sociopaths and psychopaths are separate people, which probably never crossed the mind of the person who created the hit sitcom or the 'superhero.' Most professionals believe that sociopaths and psychopaths share similar traits, and they're both housed under ASPD in the DSM (Robinson, 2014). Both disorders make people's moral compass collapse. People with both disorders don't have a normal sense of right and wrong like regular people. They both have distorted ways of thinking, and their responses to their misconduct are not similar to what can be expected from someone who follows the rules. The key difference between sociopaths and psychopaths is the extent of whether they have a conscience or not. Psychopaths are believed to have little to no conscience, but sociopaths have a weak conscience.

A psychopath doesn't have the little voice inside their heads telling them what's right and wrong. They don't feel hesitant to steal from you or physically hurt you. They don't share your emotional pain, and they won't have the conscience that makes them think twice about insulting someone's human or emotional rights. A psychopath cannot stand in your shoes, but a sociopath also struggles to see other people's perspectives or feel their pain, even though they have a weak conscience. The little voice telling them what's right and wrong isn't loud enough. A sociopath knows that hurting you is wrong, but they might do it anyway. They know that stealing is wrong, but their conscience is too weak to make them feel bad about their actions. A sociopath might even feel a hint of remorse or guilt for their behavior.

The dysfunctional conscience is a trait both types of APSD sufferers experience, but they experience it on different levels. This makes a psychopath more dangerous than a sociopath. However, as you can see from the trend in television and movies lately, neither disorder causes an indefinite violent outburst. Both conditions can lead to a violent nature, but it rarely happens. Most people with ASPD never become violent, but they can be hard to trust because they lack the normal function of a conscience. They both have similarities when it comes to being selfish and manipulative, but there are some larger differences in their traits and habits.

The Creation of Each

Psychopaths are designed by nature and have no ability to feel empathy for others, but sociopaths are more likely to be raised in an impoverished home combined with trauma and abuse. A psychopath can also experience a traumatic childhood and life that amplifies their ingrained nature, but experience is thought to be the sole creator of sociopathy. Sociopaths also have a small capacity to feel empathy for others if they try, but they tend to disregard the rights of others to promote their own cause. Violence isn't an innate characteristic of a sociopath, but they have short fuses. They can fly off the handle for little to no reason. They struggle to control their tempers. Cornering a sociopath with consequences after their behavior may well ignite violent, reactive, or enraged behavior.

A sociopath will also try to justify their behavior by any means. They'll even try to justify the choices they make before they enact the behavior. For example, a sociopath might tell themself that the world is against them and everything in their life goes wrong, so that justifies their criminal behavior. They never had the opportunities their friends had when they grew up, so they must take what was privileged to other people. No one gave them wealth like their best friend, who is coincidentally no longer a friend, so they will steal, plunder, threaten, and cheat their way to the top. A sociopath might feel entitled to a certain outcome just because other people have what they want. They don't always realize how these people worked hard for what they have.

Another example of a sociopath trying to justify their decisions is when they sexually abuse young children. They were sexually abused as a child, and they turned out 'fine.' Well, that's what their slightly broken moral compass tells them in the moment. They lose themself as they hurt a young child.

A less extreme example is when a sociopathic parent chooses to reprimand their children with corporal punishment because it's the only way kids learn in their experience. Their parents spanked them when they didn't do what was expected, so why must they parent their children any different? If confronted about this, they'll turn into a flaming ball of rage to defend what they've convinced themselves to be real or acceptable. Sociopathy is strongly related to traumatic childhood experiences, such as sexual, physical, verbal, or emotional abuse.

A sociopath might've been neglected as a child, or maybe their parents abused alcohol and drugs, leaving them to fend for themselves. Their parents might even have been abusive to each other, and they may have pulled the sociopathic child into the middle to choose sides. Psychopathy starts with underdevelopment of certain brain regions as you learned in Chapter Two, and a child's underlying traits could surface if their childhood is poor enough. This makes them the primary psychopaths. Sociopaths are the ones who suffer from an unwanted and underprivileged childhood, which makes them secondary psychopaths. Secondary psychopaths aren't as dangerous, but they might be less willing to socialize. Sociopaths could be erratic while psychopaths are more meticulous and calculating.

Diagnosing Primary and Secondary Psychopathy

It's harder to spot a psychopath than it is to recognize a sociopath. Both disorders are characterized by certain traits, which need to be present for someone to be diagnosed with ASPD. Both disorders will use specific and abnormal functional characteristics, including boosting their self-esteem with personal gain, pleasure, and power. They'll be extremely selfish, and their goals will be based on their desires and immediate personal gratification, no matter how it impacts other people's rights. Sociopaths and psychopaths will also have flawed interpersonal or personality characteristics, which are seen when they interact with other people. Sociopaths and psychopaths will show a lack of empathy toward people they hurt, manipulated, or offended, even though sociopaths can feel empathy.

They'll also both struggle to have mutually healthy relationships because they always want to control their partners. Behavioral characteristics are also investigated to diagnose someone with sociopathy or psychopathy.

People with both disorders will disregard agreements, commitments, and promises, even if they get into financial trouble. They might also be involved in repeated assaults or disagreements, and they both lie like their lives matter on it. They'll both show behavioral characteristics of manipulating people to gain entry or progress for themselves, and impulsivity is a daily habit. Other diagnosable characteristics are meanness, rage, callousness, aggression, spitefulness, sadism, and a lack of remorse when confronted for their actions.

Behavioral characteristics are used to diagnose sociopaths and psychopaths because it shows just how far they're prepared to go to manipulate, coerce, and deceive their victims. Stealing money from someone under false pretenses is deceitful. Lying to a friend to change their minds to agree with you is coercion. Misdirecting the blame for your actions to someone else is manipulation. Even though sociopathy and psychopathy have distinct differences, these traits are still used to diagnose someone under the umbrella of ASPD. However, there are major differences, and the two disorders deserve their own categories. That's why professionals refer to primary and secondary psychopathy. Some professionals are aware of the differences between sociopathy and psychopathy, but many people confuse the two.

Perhaps you or someone you know has been diagnosed with ASPD. Maybe you were lucky to be diagnosed as sociopathic or psychopathic from the start. Both disorders are a failed personality disorder that means the sufferer cannot empathize with someone else's emotions. Neither type of ASPD can relate and respond to other people's emotions. This causes an underlying inability to care about what other people need and feel. One way to recognize which ASPD disorder someone suffers from is by looking at a sociopath versus psychopath chart online. Doctor Kevin Dutton used a chart called the psychopathic personality inventory revised (PPI-R) to determine how presidential candidates were scoring as psychopaths versus known psychopaths (University of Oxford, 2016). This chart is commonly used to distinguish whether someone is sociopathic or psychopathic.

Nonetheless, the psychopathic scores of some well-known names might be surprising. Saddam Hussein obviously takes first place with a score of 189, and he's closely followed by Adolf Hitler with 169. On the same chart, we see Winston Churchill with a score of 155, George Washington with 132, and Abraham Lincoln with 123. These people have been scored for fearless dominance, self-centeredness, and cold-heartedness. It's no surprise that Hussein takes first place, but some presidents are also among those names. Even Donald Trump entered the chart in 2016 with a score of 171, which is mighty close to Hussein. Anyway, this chart made waves in the psychiatric world, but sociopathic versus psychopathic charts like the PPI-R can help you distinguish a sociopath from a psychopath.

Traditional psychotherapy isn't normally helpful for people with ASPD. However, some behaviors can be changed if the person is willing to do the work, especially in sociopaths. Psychopaths have faulty brain circuits, which might not be present in sociopaths (Khan, 2018). Counseling can be an option for anyone willing to change, even a psychopath. It might be a harder journey for them, but the intention is the start of change. Detecting the condition early in life also increases the chance of success with counseling, and there are many options available online that help with affordable mental healthcare. Remember, not all psychopaths or sociopaths will be cold-blooded killers. You may know one or there may be more you've never noticed before.

Distinct Differences

There are some vastly distinct differences between psychopaths and sociopaths. Sociopaths are also known as hot-headed while psychopaths are known as cold-blooded. The reason sociopaths are called hot-headed is that they're prone to emotional outbursts and abnormal fits of rage. Remember that both psychopaths and sociopaths can feel emotions themselves. They just struggle to distinguish and relate to other people's emotions. Sociopaths are driven by their anger, rage, and impulsivity. They're extremely disorganized and more likely to live on the outskirts of society. They don't socialize as well as psychopaths, and their inability to organize their lives, finances, and responsibilities are the reasons they fall prey to poverty or unsuccessful careers and relationships.

A sociopath also wants everything a psychopath wants, but they're too much of a loose cannon to achieve it in most cases. Sociopaths are volatile and unpredictable. Psychopaths can also be unpredictable, but they're more likely to calculate their actions before doing anything. A sociopath is so disorganized that they might even mess up when they commit crimes. Their inability to be as meticulous and pedantic as their psychopathic counterparts can make them leave clues behind for law enforcement. A sociopath is more likely to be caught, but they'll use everything they have to justify their behavior. They'll take no responsibility, and they'll defend themselves aggressively. You don't want to corner a sociopath in a thriller because they act on impulse more than anything else.

A psychopath will analyze every detail and pay attention to every step of their plan. They're pedantic and perfectionistic. They won't be caught as easily as sociopaths. They have no emotional attachment to anything or anyone. Indeed, they can love someone in their own way, but they can't form healthy bonds easily. Sociopaths are likely to have some relationships, even if they're unhealthy. The meticulous difference between sociopaths and psychopaths can also be seen in interpersonal relationships. For example, a sociopath will explode with rage when their partner confronts them about a lie. They'll use excuses to justify their lie, and they may turn themselves into a victim of circumstance. A psychopath won't easily be caught lying, but when you catch them, they'll deny it and make you question your logic.

Sociopaths are more likely to be uneducated and unsure of the direction of their lives. They'll struggle to hold down a job because their ability to plan is faulty. A sociopath might even become homeless and wander around without a purpose, but a psychopath will more likely trample their associates to reach the top of the ladder. Sadly, they may do whatever is necessary to manifest their carefully designed plan. Where psychopaths also have the benefit of not being emotional, which allows them to tenaciously and viciously pursue their dreams, sociopaths are restricted by impulsivity. A sociopath won't overthink their options, which could lead to them making the wrong decision before a second thought pops into their minds.

However, one would think sociopathy is more dangerous because of their impulsivity, but that's not true. The danger lies within the person who meticulously plans every step of their dream. Psychopaths have no emotional or moral compass, and this is what makes them more dangerous. Their ability to strategize on a higher level makes them challenging to catch in the act. And when you catch them, they probably have a long list of escape plans. Psychopathy is the most dangerous type of personality disorder, even though most psychopaths never become violent. They're hazardous in other ways, too. They can be treacherous in the workplace if they want your position. They have no emotional or empathetic attachment to what happens to you. They'll get you fired without blinking.

Worst of all is that it will happen fast and unexpectedly. They might ruin your reputation just to win. A sociopath doesn't have this kind of grit. They're messy and sloppy in their plans. Chances are they might even get themselves fired for being sloppy. When you think of a dangerous person, think cold-hearted, calm, collected, and intelligent. When you think of someone who inconveniences you, think of a hot-headed, impulsive, and self-destructive person. A psychopath's ability to be cold-blooded makes them a highly effective criminal if they choose this path. That's the secret to helping yourself or someone you love if you recognize psychopathy. You need to choose a different path. There is help and hope for you, so don't let your first choice be incriminating. The prisons are full of criminals.

It can be challenging to recognize a psychopath when they target you, especially when they switch that disabling charm on to attract you like a bug to a light. Remember that a psychopath is a predator, and you can't change their neurological design. They might be able to change it slowly and with much effort, but you can't do that for them. It's tough recognizing someone you deeply care about as a psychopath. It's even tougher to recognize yourself as one. However, understanding the way a psychopath sees the world can help in knowing whether their minds can be changed.

Chapter 5:

How Psychopaths See the World - Can You Change Them?

Seeing through the eyes of a killer is understandably not something most people would want to witness, but fortunately, most psychopaths aren't killers. Being able to understand what a psychopath sees is a vital tool for dealing with one. Only once we can see through their eyes, can we understand what makes them tick, and we can work toward finding better treatments for this disorder. You won't be looking into the sickest minds on earth, but you'll learn what research has uncovered to stride toward better treatment.

Through the Eyes of a Psychopath

Everyone sees the world differently. We all have varying perspectives about reality and life, but our perceptions are carefully guided by beliefs and ethics. The way we mature through childhood can change how we perceive the world. For example, parents who consistently convince their daughters that all boys are not to be trusted will instill beliefs that boys are generally untrustworthy. This happens over years, and it's called environmental conditioning. The society we grow up in can also change our perspectives. If we grow up in a small town where everyone is too afraid of moving to the city because the crime rates are too high, we'll likely believe we don't have what it takes to make it in the city. Every experience we have as children is designing the way we see the world.

However, a psychopath already has a faulty brain network on top of which these beliefs may pile. An unemotional child living in a society that doesn't offer support or acknowledgment of their emotions will simply believe that emotions aren't valid. Their beliefs will embed themselves deeper and deeper until they stick. Psychopaths fail to relate their actions to consequences, and this can also be amplified during childhood. They don't receive acknowledgment for doing good, and they're punished in a cruel manner when they misbehave. Either way, they lack the groundwork needed for a better belief system. It doesn't take bad parenting to instill these beliefs, either.

Psychopathic children may isolate themselves from society because they feel different.

They might practice cruel behavior behind closed doors, possibly going unnoticed for years. They may just be the bully at school, which seems harmless in some households, but this reinforces their beliefs that what they desire can be taken by force. Even giving a child everything that they demand installs poor beliefs because they know they can manipulate everyone to get what they desire in adulthood. The bottom line is that no two people can experience exactly the same childhood, so everyone's perspective is different. A psychopath's perspective is likely entirely different due to their lack of empathy, but they also have no sense of what's acceptable in society. Moreover, their neurological development lacks the construction to automatically see someone else's perspective.

Most people can see another person's perspective if they choose to see it, but psychopaths need more encouragement. It doesn't mean they can't see your perspective, it just doesn't happen naturally. Lindsay Drayton from the Department of Psychology at Yale University stepped in to research the lack of perspective adoption in psychopaths (Drayton et al., 2018). Drayton understands that psychopaths find it challenging to understand how someone else feels because they lack this innate ability. This is what makes them seem downright selfish. However, psychopaths can understand another person's beliefs, thoughts, and desires.

Drayton bravely approached the Connecticut maximum-security prison to ask if she could work with their psychopathic inmates to understand them better. She and her colleagues were deeply fascinated by how complex the psychopathic mind was, and her curiosity finally led to the prison after 10 years of research. Most people wouldn't want to work with violent psychopaths, but Drayton was an exception. She even set up a makeshift lab in the prison that only contained a desk and computer. There were no barriers between her and the psychopaths, and she didn't allow guards inside the room. Her work was confidential. She treated these inmates as regular clients. The American prison system doesn't automatically assess psychopathy when new inmates arrive.

Drayton and her team had to assess 106 inmates themselves. Only 22 male inmates tested strongly for psychopathy, 28 inmates weren't psychopathic, and the rest of them fell into an uncertain group. The 22 psychopaths proved to be narcissistic, glib, superficial, manipulative, and conniving, and these men became Drayton's main focus. These men weren't shy to share the gory details of their crimes. Drayton suspected that these men have never been given the chance to share their perspectives, albeit it was horrendous. The rest of the inmates were used as control groups to compare the results to when Drayton started testing the ability of psychopathic inmates to take on someone else's perspective. The psychopaths were then given a computer exam.

Each psychopath watched an avatar dressed in prison clothes on the screen, and the avatar would either face left or right. Red dots would then appear before and behind the avatar's line of sight. Either one dot would be behind them, two dots in front of them, and so on. The pictures would change quickly because speed was a factor in determining whether psychopaths could automatically take on the perspective of the avatar. The same test was done with control groups within the prison who didn't test positive for psychopathy. The regular inmates were quickly adept at taking the perspective of the avatar. They were asked to record the total number of red dots on the screen, and they typically recorded only what the avatar could see in their line of sight.

The same thing happened with the psychopaths, which truly intrigued Drayton and her team. The psychopaths were able to speedily take on the perspective of the avatar by counting mostly the same number of dots that could be seen by the avatar and not those that couldn't be seen. Regular people could slow down their decisions, and this will make them tally the dots the avatar can't see. This doesn't happen with speedy totals because of a thing called egocentric interference, which is the ability to relate to what the avatar sees. The dots behind the avatar will interfere with their ability to take the avatar's perspective, but the inmates could bypass this. The psychopath's egocentric interference was similar to the regular people, but their altercentric interference was different.

The altercentric interference means the psychopathic inmate's perspectives were interfering with that of the avatar. The results proved that psychopaths don't automatically adopt another person's perspective. They can deliberately see someone's perspective though. They can see your perspective because their egocentric interference works similarly to a regular person. Psychopaths are known to pay keen attention to their goals, which may influence this test. The goal is to spot the dots within the avatar's perspective, so that's what they focus on. However, psychopaths tend to ignore anything within their peripheral vision when they're focused like this. That's why they didn't care to consider that there were more dots, even though their minds knew the dots were there.

What was more interesting among the results is that psychopaths who scored higher on the psychopathy test were less responsive to the experiment, and they had more offenses on their criminal records. This may indicate that severe psychopaths don't respond to the avatar because they can't adopt the egocentric interference, meaning they will be unlikely to see someone else's perspective. This research delved into the theory of mind, which is the assessment of how much a certain person can see and feel what others do. ASPD is not the only personality disorder that shows differences in theory of mind. Asperger syndrome is a personality disorder where the development of social and communication aspects in the brain hasn't progressed well.

A study published in *Science* measured the ability of people with Asperger syndrome to mentalize with others (Senju et al., 2009). Mentalizing is also a theory of mind where people can see someone else's perspective. People with Asperger syndrome are capable of understanding someone else's beliefs and desires when asked to do so, but they also can't automatically assume someone else's viewpoint. There were 17 participants in the control group and 19 people with Asperger syndrome. The control group's eyes responded as expected when actors played their parts, but the Asperger group didn't show any spontaneous eye movements when watching the same display. These people also don't automatically anticipate what the actor will do next.

The Asperger study proved that some similarities might lie within the ability to observe and respond to someone else's reactions, albeit they're very different conditions. Not being able to anticipate pain or an emotional response from someone else's viewpoint is callous, but Asperger sufferers lack a connection between their social-communication regions in the brain. Both disorders have some neurological fault that underlines the main reason they behave the way they do. Psychopathy is a complicated concoction of genetics and environmental issues that influence the most malleable organ in the body—the brain. Long-term studies still need to assess the malleability of the brain and its processes, but Drayton proved that we can force inmates to take someone else's perspective.

Drayton's study doesn't prove that they adopt other people's emotions though. This is what needs further research. However, prison guards could start teaching inmates to see someone else's viewpoint. The bottom line is that with enough effort, psychopaths can see your perspective, but it requires concerted and deliberate effort. They need a goal, or their altercentric interference will oppose the alternative perspective.

Is Change Possible?

Change is a fragile word unless it focuses on the different types of ASPD. Sociopathy is possibly easier to treat than psychopathy because it doesn't have the neurological factor. Take Sam and Adam as an example. Sam sits on the playground, and he watches Adam who beats him at the science fair. Sam is stewing, but he's carefully devising an attack. He'll wait for Adam at the swings, and then he'll trip him while he walks past to make it look like an accident. The plan doesn't work out well for either boy. Adam trips, but he suddenly goes into a rage with Sam, punching him as the crowd gathers. The guidance counselor sees what's happening and runs toward the boys. Sam is sly, and he blames the start of the fight on Adam.

Adam is now being questioned for his involvement, but he loses it again and punches the guidance counselor as he runs away. The question now is who do we blame more, and what will help both boys control their misconduct? Sam is obviously psychopathic, but Adam is likely a sociopath. Sam uses meticulous planning, and Adam loses his temper. In fact, both boys are to blame, but the instigator is Sam, even if it will never be known to the guidance counselor. In his eyes, both boys are thrown in the same detention hall because they were equally guilty. Indeed, Adam shouldn't have lost his cool, but Sam is the dangerous one who bullied him in the first place. The reason psychopathic treatments are so immature at the moment is that they have a developmental disadvantage.

At any age, both disorders are challenging to treat, but psychopathy is the main concern. Adam's behavior will likely change when he learns how his actions lead to unwanted consequences for himself, but Sam doesn't see things the same way. The same happens in our criminal justice system. Both men in a similar scenario are probably violent, and they're being treated as the same problem, but they're completely different. Talk therapy and punishment aren't always the right incentives for psychopaths to stop their behavior. Both disorders can be violent, but throwing them in jail as one type of ASPD could be a mistake. Their brains work differently, so they require varying rehabilitation approaches. Most children will go through a stage of biting, kicking, screaming, and hurting others.

Tantrums are abundant in children, and it could indicate that a child needs special attention if it's out of control. As children, sociopaths will likely respond well to strict boundaries, reducing their risks for being sociopathic as adults. Early intervention is the key to helping both types of ASPD. Indeed, it won't be easy if a psychopath is already set in their ways, but catching it earlier than later could make all the difference. Children's brains are still developing. They have a chance at a normal life if they are guided through a supportive childhood. Children's brains are highly malleable during this time, and even a genetically psychopathic child could change. Sociopathic children who throw endless tantrums and bite their siblings could learn from their mistakes at a young age.

However, unemotional and callous children are often overlooked for seeming normal. These children are called "happy aggressives," and their parents think everything's fine because they don't seem fazed by violence, emotions, and fear like other kids. Parents think they hit the jackpot, but sometimes, a child needs to walk into a psychologist's office to make sure everything is developing as it should. Happy but aggressive children does not mean you're lucky as a parent. These children are already struggling with empathy and seeing other people's perspectives. As you learned in Chapter One, inherent psychopathy is proven to be a factor, so your child could be one long before they show signs. Catching a monster long before they become one is how you change them.

One difference seen in the brain of psychopaths is how their reward and pleasure centers function. A young or older psychopath processes rewards differently in their brain, so it would make a huge difference to focus on that to change neural networks. If you recall an earlier study, delayed gratification was also a far reach for psychopaths. They expect rewards for their behaviors immediately, even if that reward is something that would turn our stomachs. Psychopaths also process punishment differently from regular people. A psychopath feels inferior to everyone, but they exude a superiority complex like no other. They want to make you think they're better than you. They want to feel superior to you. A psychopath doesn't feel the same range of emotions you do, and this makes them fearless and dominant. Emotions are weaknesses to psychopaths.

Punishment often fails because psychopaths exude this superiority over therapists, teachers, counselors, and parents. They may even mock you to make themselves feel better. They'll also undermine someone who tries to punish them because they don't understand punishment. Their rewards and punishment wires are crossed. Their threshold for pain and negative experiences is much higher than a regular person because they don't feel stress like other people. Pain is merely a consequence of stress in many cases. Their emotions are also dormant, so they won't fear punishment. It won't deter them. Placing a group of psychopaths in one room for therapy would probably backfire. They'll feed off each other's callousness to amplify their attack against you. As such, group treatments aren't an option for psychopaths.

Punishment is not the best option for rehabilitation, either. Their reward system in the brain works in such a way that positive reinforcement of the desired behavior and thinking is potentially a better way to treat young psychopaths. Just as they don't feel or understand the pain and fear of others, they also don't understand the pleasure side of doing what's right. Introduce them to positive reinforcement, and you stand a chance of changing young psychopaths. Keeping them busy with hobbies could give them something to enforce positive feelings in their minds. Parents could also be supportive toward their children to reduce the risk of them becoming psychopathic later in life. Children with unemotional personalities are at a much greater risk of becoming psychopaths as adults.

Positive reinforcement of the desired behaviors in psychopaths could cultivate empathy. Drayton was on to something when she examined whether psychopaths could take other people's perspectives. Could this also help them to start understanding how people feel during their misconduct? A virtual reality experiment conducted by the University of Barcelona might be able to open doors for new treatments that allow psychopaths to start cultivating empathy (Geddes, 2018). The university examined domestic violence perpetrators by placing them in virtual reality scenarios where they were the vulnerable woman who was about to be attacked by a violent man. This is part of a new rehabilitation program in Barcelona, which is currently offered to first-time offenders.

The men are embodied in a virtual reality version of vulnerable women avatars, and they have to experience the attack from a woman's perspective. The aggressive male avatar in the program verbally abuses the woman before smashing a telephone against the wall. Finally, he invades her personal space and abuses her. Role-play is quite popular in therapy today, but it can't match the experience of virtual reality. The offenders are tested before and after their virtual session to see if they can recognize fear in a woman's face, and the results show that they're able to recognize it after the session. A lot of work still needs to be done before this form of rehabilitation can be widely used, but it's promising at this point. The only uncertainty is whether the results will remain with the psychopath in the long run.

The current research to understand and change the psychopathic mind shows a lot of promise. Early intervention is the best because a child's brain is still developing, making it more malleable than an adult's brain. This doesn't mean adults can't be treated, but early intervention is the best start to the changes you want to see. A willingness to change is the second key to treatment as you saw in Drayton's research. Inmates could deliberately take another person's perspective, which leads to the third key of potentially life-changing treatments—positive reinforcement. A psychopath's brain also desires rewards and pleasure, so it would help the brain reinforce positive behaviors instead of sadistic ones. Whoever you know with psychopathic traits, irrespective of their age, there is hope.

Combining medication with neurofeedback and psychotherapy to help psychopaths cultivate an understanding of people's emotions can change the world. Meanwhile, you can learn how to deal with them to avoid reinforcing the wrong behaviors and encouraging their manipulation.

Chapter 6:

How to Deal With Psychopaths and Their Weaknesses

Knowing that anyone can be a psychopath in hiding sure makes it a challenge to deal with them, but you at least know how to recognize them now. You may have coworkers who show psychopathic traits, or your best friend could be a mean and manipulative predator. Chances are that you know someone who targets you, or you deal with a psychopath in your daily routine. There are ways to deal with psychopaths that won't leave you hanging by a thread. Some psychopaths can be avoided while others can be managed to ensure your well-being and success don't take a plunge.

Three Mental Fortes

Some people think of running as soon as they identify a psychopath in their midst, especially if they've already survived the brunt of this person's narcissistic and grandiose behavior. It's always an option if you can remove yourself from the situation. No one says you have to be friends with someone who could hurt you at any moment. You don't have to tolerate the person who puts their needs before yours or devalues your emotions. However, we can't always hide from every psychopath. They walk among us, and we might work with one who is now becoming our prime suspect. Some people are fortunate to be able to change careers or companies, but chances are that they'll end up in the clutches of a new psychopath anyway. In a case where you can't avoid a psychopath at work, you need the three mental fortes.

Building your mental strength to deal with a psychopath is your best shot at thriving in your career when someone wants everything better than you have. Take a moment to think hard about the people you work with. Recognize whether there is a psychopath who makes your life difficult at work because these are the ones that we struggle to avoid. You can start building a mental stronghold against the predator by following three rules.

Rule one is to never show your weaknesses or vulnerabilities. Predators prey on your emotions, so keep them in check. Always show a calm and collective response to the person. Every time you react to their misconduct or foul nature, they'll keep coming back for more. Don't get frustrated or upset with them because this amplifies their power over you. Don't show them if you feel intimidated. They love intimidating other people with their narcissistic demeanor. Be assertive with an aggressive psychopath at work when they think they can intimidate you by standing over your shoulders or passing subtle threats. Bullying should be reported directly to human resources, but don't show any emotional response to their behavior.

Rule two is to be wary of their victimhood stories. Don't buy into their so-called pains and elaborate tales. Be cautious of someone who always blames other people for their shortfalls. A psychopath doesn't take responsibility for their actions. They want to manipulate you with their soppy dramas to gain your sympathy. Show them none. Sometimes, you have to be cold to avoid a cold-hearted attack. You can even show your disbelief by cleverly turning the tables on them. Sally complains that John is lazy because he wouldn't help her with the presentation. She always complains and makes it look like John's to blame for her missed deadline. Surprise Sally by turning the tables. Ask her whether she helped John fix his computer bug last week as he asked. Suddenly, Sally can see you're aware of both sides of the story, and she realizes she can't manipulate you.

Rule three is to switch to digital communication whenever you can. An interesting study was published in *Personality and Individual Differences* (Crossley et al., 2016). Machiavellians were the center of attention in this study. Remember that they are part of the dark triad personality types who also suffer from psychopathy and narcissism. Nonetheless, 206 subjects were part of the study, which examined the differences between computerized and face-to-face negotiations. The results offered good news because psychopaths had less influence over people when communicating digitally. Psychopaths thrive on face-to-face communications, and they can more easily manipulate you this way. Take this strength away from them, and they won't easily be able to treat you like a puppet. Online communication makes it hard for them to use their dark charm on you.

The three mental fortes will help you avoid getting hurt by the psychopaths you can't avoid, especially in the workplace. Practice them often because any mental strengthening tool must be exercised to increase your forte.

Watch Out!

Predatorial personalities all have one thing in common: They want to exploit you in any way they can. This includes narcissists, psychopaths, and sociopaths. The way they exploit you is by summing you up to find your weaknesses and vulnerabilities. Psychopaths are constantly on the prowl to find what makes you tick and use it against you. Knowing which vulnerabilities are most attractive to psychopaths could help you keep them in check. These are summaries of what you must consciously notice in your own behavior so that psychopaths don't leech off your well-being. Some weaker traits you may possess can also overlap.

Your need to feel accepted, validated, and not weird or out of place in group situations can send up a flare to attract these predators. Everyone feels the need to fit in with others to some extent, but some of us become a little neurotic about it. We become dependent on someone accepting us when we try so hard to be someone we are not. This vulnerability is a manipulator's dream because they can control you by feeding you validation when you need it and taking it away when they want to see you fold. The fear of not fitting into society makes this a weakness on which predators thrive. A predator watches whether you feed your need for approval on cue, and most people tend to become neurotic when this doesn't happen, so the psychopath steps in to take control. Consider whether you have any of these traits.

Perhaps you're over-agreeable because you fear the rejection of disagreeing with someone. Rejection is a painful reminder that you aren't accepted by the person, and a manipulator can use this to make you fit into their acceptance. Consider whether you have "people-pleaser syndrome." People who suffer from this syndrome are too afraid of rejection to involve themselves in any form of conflict, especially heated conflict. Do you fear conflict? Sometimes, you have to ask yourself difficult questions, too. Do you have a sense of vanity? There's a difference between vanity and self-esteem. Self-confidence is when you value your own worth, but vanity is when you expect others to value your worth the same way you do. A psychopath will manipulate your vanity by complimenting you sometimes, and they'll undermine your sense of self-value when they want something from you.

Start recognizing your need for approval before it's exploited. Question whether you have outright reactions to what people say about you. Do you respond excessively with your facial expressions, tone of voice, and body language? Your tonality is giving your vulnerability away. You need more of a "who cares" attitude when people say things about you. Even the fear of standing out when you speak up about a psychopath's behavior is a sign of approval-seeking. You have to be cautious of displaying your emotional responses when a psychopath compliments or undermines you, and don't be afraid to stand your ground. Assertiveness and a willingness to support your authentic ideas can scare them off. If you're oversensitive about societal validation, a psychopath can offer and remove it on cue to control your emotional and psychological well-being.

Setting poor self-boundaries can also attract predators. Abusive relationships often come back to a lack of personal boundaries that allow the perpetrator to continue their behavior. Constantly doubting your boundaries, decisions, beliefs, morals, and reality can also unravel your mind to a psychopath. It opens you up to receive manipulation and exploitation by not asserting what you strongly believe to be true. Being uncertain of your perspectives can already be a sign that a predator has clawed their way into your life. Remember that psychopaths have a way of making you question your thoughts, emotions, and reality. Not setting boundaries in place to protect yourself and your mind can allow psychopaths to use the popular gaslighting technique to exploit your free nature. They'll gaslight your reality until you don't believe it anymore.

Once you question your reality and the truth, a psychopath has full control over you, and they can abuse or manipulate you as they wish. The lack of personal boundaries is one of the reasons abused victims return to their abusers. The missing boundary, in this case, is allowing the psychopath back into your life. Trust me, they'll try their utmost best to persuade you that you need them. There are a few ways psychopaths can exploit this weakness. They might move in with you before you even know them, which doesn't allow you enough time to see their psychopathy. They might also invade your personal and mental space with prying questions to know you better. These questions would normally make you feel uncomfortable at first. Abusive patterns might become prevalent, but you'll be questioning your reality at this stage already, making you wonder if it's really abuse.

The psychopath will begin their twisted truths to make you doubt yourself even more. They'll blame you for their actions, and you'll be too vulnerable to question whether they're gaslighting you. This is how they start breaking down your self-esteem, confidence, and personal privacy. Everyone deserves some privacy, even in romantic relationships. What makes this worse is that the unacceptable behavior will increase gradually, making it hard to recognize until you're in a pit. You'll continue to tolerate it, and the self-doubt will multiply, leaving you stuck in a space you aren't sure is unacceptable. It's at this point you might return to them after separation because you're not sure why you booted them. After all, everyone makes mistakes, right?

That leads to the third vulnerability psychopaths look for in targets. They tend to target people who strongly believe in unconditional love. Once you know that sick-minded people exist, it's naïve to think unconditional love exists in the same world. Is it worth loving a psychopath? Everyone makes mistakes, and we all have flaws because imperfection is a beautiful thing, but we learn from our mistakes. Psychopaths don't learn from their mistakes because they don't even take responsibility for them. A lesson can't be taught when someone doesn't have remorse for their actions. That's the difference, and it explains why unconditional love is a fallacy. We always need to have the strength and knowledge to leave a toxic relationship if we aren't getting anything in return. The give-and-take relationship must exist, or you must leave.

No one should be loved and forgiven, irrespective of their inhumane treatments and habits. You'll be a neon sign calling all psychopaths if you practice unconditional love. They automatically assume they can do whatever they want to you, and you'll just forgive and love them again. This opens you up to a host of exploitations, and psychopaths will line your door with their superficial charm. The only way to show how your love is conditional with anyone in life is to set healthy personal boundaries. You should be able to say "enough is enough" when your partner, friend, or relative behaves unacceptably. Ask yourself, what is unacceptable? What would you not allow in your personal or professional life? Anyone who repeatedly transgresses against your boundaries should be cut from your circle. This will send the right message that you're not vulnerable.

Another weakness sought by psychopaths is unresolved childhood trauma, which can leave you with low self-esteem and the persistent pursuit of validation. This rings the bells of psychopaths. You may become a codependent personality type, or you can become a people-pleaser, both of which leave your wounds open for the world to see. Not addressing the traumas that you experienced in childhood makes you omit the personal boundaries you need in adulthood. You always had to fight to get attention as a child. Your parents were negligent, and they never encouraged any self-esteem. Your teachers expected the world from you, and they didn't reinforce your unique nature, turning you into a sheep that seeks the approval of society. Perhaps your father sexually abused you, and it was the only way you got attention in the home.

Now, you have no boundaries about what you'll allow in the bedroom. You're promiscuous and allow men to do whatever they want. You also constantly seek the approval of others by doing everything they ask because you were neglected as a child. A psychopath walks into your life, and they exploit every missing boundary they can find. They'll make you do things that should be questionable, and they'll offer you no love in return for yours. Anyone who didn't have proper boundary modeling in childhood could fall prey to the predator waiting to manipulate their weaknesses. Our parents should set boundaries that let us know where we begin and end. These boundaries should show us what's acceptable and unacceptable. A codependent personality will attract predators because they know you'll do anything for validation. They'll use you and your lack of boundaries to progress themselves.

Invisible wounds need to be addressed, people-pleasing must die, and healthy boundaries must be set for you to avoid the fallout a psychopath brings to your life and well-being. There's one more vulnerability they can exploit. Some people have a 'fixer' mindset. They believe they can fix someone else, including people who behave antisocially. Consider whether you still think people are innately good. Not everyone is good, and people like John Wayne Gacy and Ted Bundy have proven it. Some people are bad to their cores, and there may be hope for the milder psychopaths among us, but only they can change themselves. You can't fix them as much as you want to. Remember that unconditional love is a weakness, so you don't have to accept their flaws while thinking you can turn them around.

Be careful of behaving like a 'fixer' because psychopaths will promise you the world, but they'll be carefully planning their exploitation of your good nature. Kindness isn't the answer to dealing with a psychopath because they see it as a vulnerability. Only be kind to those who are consistently kind to you. Being conscious of your potential vulnerability attractions can help you work on them, but there are ways to deal with toxic, manipulative people.

Five Secrets of Dealing With Psychopaths

What remains a fact is that we can't avoid dealing with psychopaths, but we can control and manage the frequency in which we deal with them. We can also manage the way we address them to ensure they don't latch onto us. Even companies can start using structured interviews to assess their employees better. A psychopath is a seasoned liar, and they'll use their charm to manipulate you if you allow them enough room in a casual interview. Moreover, you should be double- and triple-checking their references because they lie so much. You may have broader options for dealing with psychopaths in your personal life as long as you stick to your guns. Five secrets exist that should determine how you deal with a predator.

The first secret isn't as hush as it seems. What do you do with a predator or a psychopath? You don't deal with them. You don't manage or control them. You don't try to change them, and you don't have relationships with them. In fact, you run for the hills and avoid them every way you can. However, this isn't always possible in the workplace. It's easier to ditch a manipulator in your personal life, but you can't always jump ship in your career. You can still apply the "don't game" to predators at work if you can't avoid them. Don't play their games, don't give them what they seek, and don't play into their victimhood. Don't see yourself as a hero who manages the psychopath at work.

You'll be headed straight into an ambush. They know the game better than you do. They've been at this their whole lives. You can't outsmart them with their skillful nature. It's like trying to win a game of poker when you have no cards in your hand. They've spent years gathering the cards they hold, and they've perfected their poker face. Besides, you don't want to stoop to their levels anyway. You're better than that. Chances are you'll more easily become them that outsmart them. Apply the "don't game" to your life to avoid psychopaths.

The second secret is to accept that some people are innately psychopathic and have no conscience. The unredeemable cannot be redeemed, no matter what you think. Not everyone is capable of being a better person. Some people are evil, others are cruel, and some are even murderous. You can't control what they think, so don't assume you can change their thoughts and behaviors. The best shot you have against a predator is to know them inside out so you can protect yourself. A psychopath is an expert at summing you up, even more than you can delve into your own authenticity. Don't let them use this against you. They can see kind-hearted and tolerant people from a mile away. Accept that they're designed to be predators. They're designed to think in ways we can't fathom to be rational.

The third secret is to uncover your vulnerabilities. Don't be afraid to dig deep because a psychopath will go deeper than you can imagine. Know what makes you most vulnerable, and work on strengthening yourself to avoid the afterburn of a psychopath. They may not hurt you physically, but they'll do everything to change your psychological well-being. Give yourself the armor you need to be resilient against their faulty nature.

The fourth secret is to distinguish lies from honest mistakes. Everyone accidentally messes up by sharing a rumor or gossiping about their colleague. However, they learn a lesson when the colleague is hurt by this rumor. Psychopaths don't learn lessons. They're pathological liars, and they can't be trusted. Psychopaths even look for victims they can use to cover their own tracks by sharing untruthful rumors to avoid getting into trouble themselves. This is often a way for them to hide their questionable behaviors once someone notices them. They simply shift the focus to a colleague by turning their reputation bad. Martha Stout from Harvard University has a system she called "rules of threes" (Barker, 2016). The first lie is probably a mistake, the second one may be a serious mistake, but the third one speaks loudly about someone.

Repeating the same habit three or more times could indicate that someone is a pathological liar. Don't trust them. What you need to do to protect yourself from this pathological habit is to boost your own reputation at work and in social circles. People tend to believe those with whom they have a good rapport. Your psychopathic friend or colleague is building a strong rapport with their charm and manipulation from day one, so make sure you're in the good books of who you might need support from when a psychopath turns on you. You don't want to be the colleague whose reputation is destroyed because of pathological lying, but you also don't want to be known as the company complainer. Building trust and a good reputation at work will design a support network when you need it the most.

You want people to believe you, and that normally happens best when you have an exceptional reputation for being prompt, reliable, trustworthy, and hard-working. Among friends, your reputation should also exceed that of the psychopath, or at least you should have a similar repertoire. Instead of investing all your energy in trying to convince people that a psychopath is on the loose, rather spend it on building a great reputation and relationship with those who will support you in a showdown.

The final secret to deal with a psychopath is by offering them a win-win situation when nothing else can work. Psychopaths love winning. It's in their aggressive personality. Negotiating with an aggressive psychopath who wants to dominate everything, offer them a win-

win solution that benefits both of you. This is also a powerful personal empowerment tool when you deal with people who don't think the same way you do. A psychopath won't feel the need to be ruthless if you can propose working together for a mutually beneficial outcome. Give them the option to get what they want as long as both of you can agree on the direction of your project if you're at work. Who knows? You might learn something valuable about using fearlessness to achieve greater success. However, use this as a last resort. Playing the "don't game" is better than negotiating with a psychopath.

If you're stuck working with one, or you have no option but to accept the psychopathic person in your life, then you can learn about the potentially beneficial qualities they have. They're not all criminals. Some of them are quite successful.

Chapter 7:

Are All Psychopaths Criminals?

You can't study frozen water alone if you want to know every property, purpose, and application of water. The problem with the misconceptions of psychopathy is that scientists mainly focus on examining the psychopaths who have already turned ice-cold. What about the psychopaths flowing freely in a society like interwoven rivers? Many of the misconceptions about psychopathy are based on the shortage of research within the regular population. Uncovering the truths about controversially successful psychopaths could show us how their free-flowing form could be empowering empires, much like strong rivers generating power.

Classical Versus Successful Psychopathy

To know if all psychopaths are criminals, one must investigate the difference between a classical and successful psychopath. Not every psychopath you meet will have a white hockey mask over their face. Not all of them will tell you gory stories of how they sliced someone into pieces. You're forgetting about their charm and tendency to lie through their teeth. Some psychopaths may seem as normal as anyone else, and they could even be successful beyond our wildest dreams. Professor of psychology Scott Lilienfeld and his young associate Ashely Watts from Emory University have reviewed the potential differences between classical and successful psychopaths (Watts & Lilienfeld, 2016). The review starts with a famous man who strikes controversy himself.

Tom Skeyhill was acclaimed to be an Australian war hero, also commonly known as the "blind soldier-poet." Skeyhill was a flag-signaler at the Battle of Gallipoli during the First World War. He wasn't in this position for long before a bomb detonated close by, blinding him. He was immediately transferred out of the war, and he wrote a poetry book that related to his combat experience. Skeyhill then toured America and other countries to share his poetry. He claimed to have met Mussolini and Vladimir Lenin, but history shows that he definitely met president Theodore Roosevelt, who even claimed to be proud of meeting the poet on stage. Ironically, Roosevelt was the highest-scoring president for psychopathy traits, such as boldness, fearlessness, and forcible relentlessness.

Anyway, Skeyhill's eyes miraculously healed after a so-called procedure in America, of which there is no proven record. Jeff Brownrigg later wrote his biography, and to everyone's surprise, Skeyhill had faked his blindness. Now that's what you call pathological lying. He maintained his lie for years, and he even managed to get away from the war. His reasons were undoubtedly selfish, but he became a successful psychopath. He escaped being caught for his lies while he built his reputation into something one of our most beloved presidents admired. That is how you fool a crowd. No tests were conducted on Skeyhill for psychopathy, but his innate ability to live a lie for that long so he could gain sympathy and manipulate people is undeniably psychopathic.

Psychopaths are indeed more likely to commit crimes than regular people, but successful psychopathy, as controversial as it seems, is not a new idea. American psychiatrist Herman Cleckley wrote *The Mask of Sanity* in 1941, and he highlighted the possibility of successful psychopaths. Cleckley explained that a psychopath is someone who exudes normalcy but hides a deeply rooted evil inside of them. They're callous, guiltless, and manipulative, but they have few interpersonal relationships that matter. This makes it hard for people to recognize their questionable behavior. Cleckley also believed that some psychopaths might hide in plain sight. They may be married to the most desirable women, and they have the highest positions in their careers.

Many people could use their psychopathic traits to achieve great things, especially in professional, political, and other empowering positions. The main reason why successful psychopathy is controversial is that scientists and scholars keep focusing on the criminals we have behind bars. What about broadening the research to include successful people who often go unnoticed for years? Some psychopaths have a smidge of impulse control and social anxiety that keeps them under the radar. No one notices them unless they mess up. The ones who mess up are the criminals behind bars. A study published in the *Journal of Abnormal Psychology* provides evidence that psychopaths are socially anxious enough to stay out of the spotlight (Ishikawa et al., 2001). The study included 26 men from an employment agency in Los Angeles and compared them to 13 convicted psychopaths.

The outsiders in the study were also assessed and found to possess psychopathic traits. Each participant had to record a video of their personal flaws, and the 26 outsiders showed an increased heart rate and blood pressure compared to the convicted psychopaths. This proves that they're more socially anxious, which may keep them out of sight in the real world. These same men performed better with an impulse regulation task than their convicted counterparts, meaning that they might mildly be capable of controlling their impulsivity. This could explain why they haven't been caught. They don't get into trouble because they're too anxious to form interpersonal relationships, and they have some control over their impulsiveness. The 26 men were formally categorized as successful psychopaths after the study.

Combine tenacious ambitions with relentless and selfish goals, and you end up with many successful psychopaths in politics, law enforcement, business, high-risk sports, and military services. After all, who would question the people you kill in a war? The review at Emory University by Watts and Lilienfeld also includes a study they conducted themselves. The trait they focused on was boldness, which naturally comes from being fearless. Boldness translates to a charming demeanor under pressure while being prepared to take risks and bounce back from stumbles. Emotional resilience is part of being brave or bold. Not every psychopath is bold, but their fearlessness predisposes them to be more likely to have the trait. The research concluded that boldness is a stepping stone to taking up a leadership role or management position.

The research surrounding boldness in psychopaths also found an association with improved presidential performance. Roosevelt performed well, but that doesn't mean he was violently psychopathic. Washington also scored high on the PPI, but he did great things. Boldness could be a positive characteristic to possess as a leader. The bold presidents weren't pathologically insane. They were aggressive enough to be the leaders we know. Leadership isn't a fun and simple game. It's challenging, and their mild psychopathic traits might've made them as successful as they were. The same research by Emory University didn't focus on impulsivity or callousness. Classical psychopaths are likely the bigger threat, but successful psychopaths can go unnoticed.

Functional Psychopaths

It's funny how a little research and knowledge can paint history an entirely different shade. You might be thinking of how many successful psychopaths made history. Well, the truth is that ancient scriptures from Rome, China, and even the Bible are packed with people who would make you cringe once you know about successful psychopaths. Sure, some leaders were outright evil, but some of them might only ping your radar now. Not every psychopath is a murderous monster. Not every predator is a rapist, killer, or thief. Some people prey subtly on your emotions and psyche, and they influence your votes, beliefs, and decisions. Psychopaths are so charmingly manipulative that we end up rooting for them in movies.

Millions of viewers turned their televisions on in 2014 when Channel Four aired the infamous *Psychopath Night*. People love the thrill of watching interviews with serial killers. We turn to bookstores to buy a pile of true-crime dramas because there's no shortage of them. Who can remove their eyes from the media coverage when a psychopathic killer is caught? Some people even misunderstand the concept of psychosis, and they think psychopathic killers are these psychotic villains. Psychosis is, in fact, a different mental disorder, and it's often temporary. Psychotic people have hallucinations, hear voices, and see what doesn't exist. They also suffer from delusions where they believe facts that aren't real.

Psychopathy is nothing like psychosis. A psychopath is fully aware and conscious of everything they do. They look like normal people, and they aren't constantly violent. They tend to win us over with their charm, making us cheer them on when we watch movies. Psychopaths are manipulative people who constantly engage in unethical, criminal, or irresponsible behaviors, according to Hare who created the PCL-R. You have conservative people who use the PCL-R test to determine if someone is a psychopath, but they rely on people who express repeated behaviors that are noticed by the public. These are the people who think only one in every 200 people in the world are psychopathic (McWilliams, 2015).

That would mean there are only 30 million global psychopaths. Indeed, about 35 percent of prisoners are psychopathic, but that doesn't mean all criminals are psychopaths or all psychopaths are criminals. Many psychopaths function normally in society, and that makes us wonder if the estimates can be trusted. Shouldn't there be more research among regular people? If you keep researching the prisoners incarcerated for violent crimes, chances are that you'll find many psychopaths. Chances are also that you'll find some who don't match the criteria, especially if you broaden your scope. Some psychopaths live to have impressive careers. What psychopaths lack is emotional intelligence, but their intelligence quotient (IQ) is normal or above-average.

The lack of emotional intelligence is commonly related to an unhealthy childhood combined with their genetic predisposition. In sociopaths, childhood influence is the core reason these people have no emotional intelligence. The shortage of evidence is largely to blame for psychopathy not being medicalized as a regular disorder like depression and autism. Research is also too infant to promise effective treatment. However, one cannot call psychopaths killers unless every psychopath was convicted of a heinous crime. Not every depressed person cries, and not every anxious person shows their nervousness. Normalize psychopathy as a common disorder that may affect those who become largely successful, and you won't be questioning whether each one of them is criminal.

Study the vast spectrum of psychopaths before making a decision. One study of 100 university students published in the *Journal of Research in Personality* proved just how complicated this conclusion might be (Mahmut et al., 2008). The students completed self-report questionnaires to compare four key aspects of psychopathy to violent criminals. The four aspects were grandiosity, impulsivity, delinquency, and a lack of empathy. The same students were then given a standard psychopathy test to determine what they would score. Comparing the results was profoundly interesting. The top 33 percent of students who scored high on the test were also self-reporting the four factors that show psychopathy. The bottom 33 percent of students also matched their psychopathy test to their self-report.

The top and bottom groups of psychopathy students were then assessed using the same methods forensic psychotherapists use on violent criminals to see if their empathy or changed perspective will show the same results as the people behind bars. Processing the same tasks as criminals would, the top 33 percent of students also failed to show empathy on a task called the Iowa Card Gambling Task. The bottom 33 percent of students matched the empathy shown by non-psychopaths. The gambling task measures activity in the orbitofrontal cortex, which is connected to decision-making and emotions. Interestingly, the high-scoring PCL-R students also showed normal executive functioning and intelligence, irrespective of their similarities to violent criminals.

The study on students proves that violent and non-violent psychopaths have the same neuropsychological processing. The researchers believe that violent psychopaths are merely a consequence of their history and childhood. They weren't supervised or supported, so they turned to criminal activities, some of which were murder. Learning more about what separates violent and non-violent psychopaths is crucial in research because it could pave the way to preventing them from becoming violent or criminal.

A child's behavior is often the byproduct of what their parents teach them, even if they have neurological deficits. Having an incarcerated parent could make a child believe criminal activities are normal. Having a parent who abuses a child could make them think it's okay to hurt other people. Having no support from your parents could turn you into someone who has no empathy toward others. It often comes back to parenting and how people were supported during childhood. A psychopath's brain may be faulty but caught early enough, the child can be guided and helped to become someone other than a killer, thief, or rapist. Anyway, functional psychopaths exist, and they can teach us how to better manage violent psychopaths or prevent them from occurring altogether. Much research is still needed, but the argument is still not over.

Murderers and Psychopaths

Thinking all psychopaths are violent and murderous might be a falsehood, but is it fair that we call all murderers psychopaths? There are two sides to every argument. It's incredible if we can prove that not all psychopaths are criminals. It's important to know that some psychopaths function better than most people. However, there's a stigma around murderers, and it's often caused by the media who don't know the true qualities of a psychopath.

The media doesn't always do their research as they should. They're quick to echo when a man did what he thought was his only option in a heated situation.

Suddenly, the man who protected his family with the only weapon he could reach is a psychopath. The media doesn't focus on how he only had a baseball bat next to his bed. No, they focus on how he smashed the guy's brains in, and they don't tell you how the guy stood over his wife with a knife in his hand. What about the wife who defended herself against her psychotic husband with a shotgun? The media sensationalizes the fact that she blasted him from two feet away, but does anyone think she had no other option? It was her life or his.

Calling all murderers psychopaths is the media's way of pretending to be knowledgeable about the disorder. What's next? The media will start calling the guy who accidentally killed a homeless man in the dark of the night around the sharpest bend a psychopath. This man was sentenced with a charge of manslaughter because he never premeditated his actions. He didn't plan to take a life, but he was unlucky to do so.

Indeed, many murderers might be psychopathic. Not every murderer is tested on the PCL-R unless they're suspected to be psychopathic. This causes another gray area where people wrongly assume that psychopaths are similar to every thief being a kleptomaniac. This happens because everyone thinks they know the facts about a disorder. Kleptomania is a disease of the mind. It has nothing to do with someone who steals bread because they're starving. The problem with psychopathy is that it's wrongly been categorized as the most malevolent disorder. Undoubtedly, psychopaths are dangerous, but there isn't enough evidence to prove that every psychopath is violent or that every murderer is a psychopath. Labeling every psychopath as a murderer prevents them from feeling socially accepted.

Labeling every murderer as a psychopath is merely the result of the media, popular culture, books, movies, and fictional characters. Expert Scott McGreal (2018) reviewed the debate as to whether all murderers are psychopaths. The debate of whether all violent people and all murderers are psychopaths stems from the misunderstanding of what makes a psychopath. The best way to measure someone's psychopathy is the PCL-R test. There's no debate about whether psychopaths can be more violent than other people. They can be criminal masterminds in some cases, and they do have a higher risk of reoffending than normal people.

A psychopathic criminal is also more likely to repeat their crimes than a criminal who doesn't score high on the psychopathy tests. Their callousness and manipulative nature make them more dangerous than the poor guy caught stealing food. Their lack of empathy makes them more willing to hurt someone else because they don't feel emotions the way normal people do. They don't see fear in someone's eyes, and they don't hear their victim's voice crack up when the psychopath says something hurtful. Their impulsivity can also be to blame, especially among psychopaths who have no control over their impulses. These are facts, but they're the only known traits amplified by the media. The media never speaks about functional psychopaths.

They don't tell you about the qualities they possess, such as bravery and high intelligence. Well, some of them are highly intelligent. The truth is that only a professional can diagnose a psychopath as one. The media aren't educated in forensic psychology, so they can't determine if someone is a psychopath. What McGreal finds most interesting is that the cut-off for psychopathy on the PCL-R test also differs regionally. North Americans use a score of 30 to diagnose someone as psychopathic, but 25 is enough to diagnose them in Europe and the United Kingdom (UK). This also confuses the matter further. The cut-off score is used to determine the number of psychopaths in a certain population. The one percent population estimate is based on a score of 30 or more.

Europe uses a continuous population estimation approach. That means they consider mild, moderate, and severe psychopaths. This allows them to determine how many functional psychopaths are about. A score between 20 and 25 is a moderate psychopath. Hare proposed that regular people will score five on his test, so that leaves a lot of room for mild and moderate psychopaths. A meta-analysis of 22 studies showed just how broad this room is for mild and moderate psychopaths among murderers (Fox & DeLisi, 2019). Juvenile and adult murderers scored between 9.4 and 31.5 on the PCL-R test. The average score appeared to be 21.1, which means that most murderers are moderately psychopathic. Some of them aren't psychopathic at all, and others are mild psychopaths.

The meta-analysis proved that only 34 percent of murderers could be classified as psychopaths if the cut-off score was 25. This number drops to 27 percent if the cut-off score is 30. These studies show that only roughly a third of murderers can officially be called psychopaths. This still poses a strong risk for homicide. Psychopathy is a high risk for violent crimes, but the more violent crimes tend to be among those with exceedingly high psychopathic scores. Criminals also tend to naturally have more psychopathic traits than regular people, so they might score above Hare's suggested five, but the fact is that not all murderers are called psychopaths, according to years of research and evidence. A lack of empathy might be the biggest problem that causes conflicting misconceptions.

The stigma is just another myth conjured by the media, and it makes functional psychopaths not want to expose themselves. Shining a light on how cruel and malevolent psychopaths can be, emphasis on the word 'can,' doesn't make it easier to research successful psychopaths. However, they do exist, and there's no doubt they have qualities that differentiate them from violent psychopaths.

A study conducted by Virginia Commonwealth University confirms what differentiates a violent and successful psychopath (McNeill, 2020). Many psychopaths can willingly refrain from violent or antisocial behavior. More than 1,000 serious juvenile delinquents were used to determine what makes a successful psychopath. Indeed, studying delinquents may seem counterproductive, but they were the basis of a longitudinal study where researchers could follow the trajectory of their lives. Secondly, they were also adolescents, and this is when the main development of impulse control happens. To control your impulses, you need to be conscientious of your traits and habits. The juveniles who tested high for psychopathic traits like grandiosity and manipulation were the ones who had successful trajectories over time. They were more conscientious of their habits and characteristics, which allowed them to control their antisocial impulses. The psychopaths who scored high initially were able to inhibit their impulsiveness to the best degree. These are the young guns who grew into careers like lawyers and chief executive officers (CEOs).

The findings from this study could prove useful in clinical and forensic settings, which could also encourage the expansion of research into successful psychopathy. To be classified as a successful psychopath, one needs to be conscientious enough to inhibit the worst antisocial behaviors so the underlying psychopathic traits can be used to achieve success instead of incarceration. Psychopaths might have strengths and qualities that could also be used to prevent their fall into the arms of criminal activities. If we could teach every psychopath that their unrelenting and tenacious behavior could benefit them instead of violent behavior followed by the justice system, we may have a way to bring the numbers down. The stigma that prevents successful psychopaths from seeking assistance is the greatest barrier.

Recognizing a child with psychopathic traits at an early age could change the trajectory of their disorder. Identifying yourself as a psychopath and seeking help could change your diagnosis from a classical to a successful psychopath. Psychopathy isn't the end of the road. It's potentially the beginning of a successful life if it's addressed. Don't hide from what can't be repressed. Rather, determine if you're a psychopath so you can do something about it, even if you just become more conscientious of your habits.

Chapter 8:

Am I a Psychopath?

This is a question few people are willing to ask themselves for the fear of finding out they might be psychopathic. However, being anxious already adds doubt to whether you're a psychopath because they don't fear things. Determining your own psychopathy won't be the easiest task, but it can help you work toward being a successful psychopath instead of a murderous one. It's time to take a few adapted tests to see whether you may need to visit an expert. Please note that you can't diagnose yourself, but you can use these simple tests and facts to determine whether you need to seek help from a professional.

Psychopathy Test

Buying this book is already a sign that you're suspicious of your traits or maybe you're worried about someone you love. This test is a loosely adapted version of psychopathy tests, which is similar to the famous PCL-R. The test is best used for anyone over the age of 18, but remember not to consider this a formal diagnosis. Only a professional mental healthcare worker can assertively diagnose psychopathy. A professional will combine a test similar to this with a structured interview with a history of your potential criminal activities and delinquency. They know what they're doing, so don't beat yourself up for being psychopathic when you're using an adapted test.

This test is structured similarly to the PCL-R, so you'll have to rate each of the 20 statements between zero and two. If the statement doesn't apply to you at all, you must rate it zero. If the statement applies loosely to you, rate it one. You may give a score of one to a statement that happens sometimes in your life. Sometimes, you're selfish, or perhaps you're occasionally unemotional. However, any statement that seems to be a persistent habit you experience should be rated two. You'll tally your score between zero and 40 after all 20 statements, and this will give you an idea of whether you should visit an expert for further examination. Use these statements to score yourself.

"I feel shallow, insincere, glib, or superficial." Are you a deep person who means what they say, or are you unfazed by promises made? This shows whether you're sincere in promises or commitments. Being insincere could mean you're using promises just to manipulate people.

"My sense of self-worth is exaggerated." Do people often think you're smug because your self-esteem borders on arrogance, or do you have sensible confidence in your worth? Having a sense of grandiosity could be a sign of pathological selfishness.

"I easily get bored and need stimulation." How often do you find yourself feeling bored, or do you always find something interesting with which to keep yourself busy? A constantly bored mind is a potential personality trait of psychopathy.

"I feel the need to lie to make things go smoother." Do you find yourself lying often, or can you still count the lies you've told? Manipulation is one of the main signs of psychopathy. Everyone lies from time to time, but score yourself according to the frequency and reasons for your lies. They could be manipulative.

"I'm a cheater who manipulates people to get my way." How do you feel when things don't go your way, and what will you be prepared to do to change the direction of things? Being dishonest by manipulating people and experiences shows that you don't follow the rules. How often do you do this? Score yourself accordingly.

"I don't often feel guilty or remorseful for what I do." Do you feel bad about letting your partner down, or do you consider your desires more important than her needs? Not allowing her to unload her emotional baggage before you ravage her could be a sign of psychopathy. Consider how often you put your desires before other people's needs. Being unable to feel guilt and remorse for hurting other people's feelings should also be calculated into your chosen rating.

"I don't easily connect emotionally with other people." How many meaningful and emotional connections do you have to others, or are you a hobbit? This statement could indicate a shallow effect or an unemotional person.

"I'm callous and don't feel empathy for others." Do you find yourself relating to someone's pain, or do you think they're being inconsiderate of your happiness when they mention their pain? Callousness and a lack of empathy toward people who need you or those who you harm should score a two.

"I'm able to earn money myself, but I like living off other people." Are you financially independent, or do you expect everyone else to fend for you? Psychopaths are highly parasitic, and they'll likely move between jobs or be homeless. Functional psychopaths might even pretend to be impoverished when they have money so others will pay their way.

"I'm impatient, easily annoyed, and I can't control my temper." Consider how much of a hot-head you are, or maybe you're impatient when you try to complete tasks. Hot-headedness is a sign of sociopathy, but it can also indicate a lack of impulse control in psychopathy.

"I'm sexually promiscuous." How often do you do things that others wouldn't try? Are you also the kind of person who sleeps with multiple partners every week? This signals a warning because it's a form of antisocial behavior.

"I gave my parents a run for their money before age 12." Were you a child who consistently got into trouble? Did you break the rules all the time, and were you ever formally reprimanded for this? Were you cruel to animals? Did you set fires? Did you vandalize other people's property, steal, cheat, and lie as a child? Perhaps you ran away from home or became sexually active before 12. These are all red flags, and you can rate yourself two.

"I don't think much about the future." A lack of long-term realistic goals indicates that you don't fear what's to come. You don't worry about tomorrow, and a lack of fear could indicate psychopathy.

"I don't think twice before I do something." This is another way for you to score your impulsivity. How often do you act on whims without thinking about them?

"I'm an irresponsible person who has no sense of loyalty or duty to friends, colleagues, and family." Thinking you owe the world nothing is another way to be selfish and lack remorse for what your actions do to others. It may also indicate how your sense of self is too grandiose, and you might have a problem with empathy.

"I find ways to rationalize my behavior, and I don't take responsibility for my actions." Consider how often you refuse to take responsibility or use excuses to rationalize your behavior. Do you find reasons to explain your behavior, or do you apologize for hurting someone?

"I cycle through many interpersonal relationships, and problems frequently arise." Ask yourself if you've had more than three relationships with romantic partners before you turned 30? If so, you'll have to score yourself two for this one.

"I was a juvenile delinquent." Have you met the formal justice system before the age of 17? Again, this statement measures your probability of being highly antisocial as a child.

"I revoked a serious condition." Perhaps you escaped from an institution, or you broke your parole or probation conditions. Any major escape or broken condition with the law automatically rates this statement as a two.

"I brush with the law often as an adult." How many parking tickets have you collected? Have you ever stolen anything, even just a candy bar? Have you run a red light before? Even minor brushes with the law count toward this rating. Six brushes of any kind earns a two-star rating here.

Calculate your total score after rating each statement between zero and two. This gives you an idea of whether you might be a psychopath or not. If you end up with a score higher than 20, please seek help from an expert. Get a proper diagnosis so you can become a successful psychopath. Moreover, you'll also reduce the risks of hurting people you may love.

Self-Assessment for Psychopathy

There are a few adapted self-assessments online you can use to measure your psychopathic or narcissistic traits. However, they all warn that you shouldn't consider them to be a diagnosis. This is another test adapted from the PCL-R and the DSM to determine whether you have the traits. These questions may seem more forward, and you must rate them honestly. No one is watching you, so you can be honest with yourself. The ratings will work similarly to the last test, but this one only has 10 statements. You'll also rate zero if a statement doesn't apply to you, one if it applies somewhat, and two if it applies to much of your life. Your total score for this self-assessment will only be out of 20, which can then be doubled to get your psychopathy score as per the PCL-R. The statements are as follows:

"I'm a smooth-talking, shallow, sly, albeit charming person. I exude a confident and self-assured impression on people, and I'm not easily left speechless. I can talk over anyone."

"I'm a self-centered, self-assured, and highly opinionated braggart. I'm cocky beyond most people, and I believe I can do anything, no matter how risky it may be."

"I can be as sly as a fox and as shrewd as a serpent. I'm more crafty, rational, and intelligent than other people.

I'm also capable of being underhanded, untrustworthy, and unscrupulous when I want something bad enough. I'm manipulative and deceitful because my desires matter more than other people's needs. Dishonesty is a good friend of mine."

"I've frequently used deception to cheat people in my life. My deceit has conned or defrauded others out of money, possessions, or even beliefs. I don't really care about the suffering of others, so I'll use deception to improve my life and wealth."

"Other people's suffering and losses caused by me don't phase me. Some people just deserve the brunt they suffer because they're dull, unintelligent, or weak. Their behavior toward me also justifies what I did to them. I cannot feel for the people I leave in my wake."

"People love telling me how cold-hearted I am. I'm a gregariously social creature who sneakily involves myself in other people's business, just so I can offer them nothing, especially support. I don't feel warm inside when I'm surrounded by these people. I feel a sense of neutrality toward my social group. If I feel anything more, it often passes quickly. These feelings can also create self-conflict when my interests are ignored."

"I would declare that I lack feelings for other people. Many people call me tactless, cold, unemotional, and inconsiderate. I don't understand what's wrong with these people."

"The sun will shine at midnight before I take responsibility for my actions. I'd rather manipulate someone else or blame anyone other than myself. I'll do anything to divert the attention away from my imperfections."

"Sometimes, I yearn for exciting, adventurous, and thrilling stimulation. I get bored too easily, so I need something to keep me busy, irrespective of whether it's a huge risk. I love taking chances and behaving in risky manners. Being in the same job for too long or completing a long and boring task seems like too much of my precious time wasted. I'd rather lead an adventurous life, even if it's dangerous."

"Much of the money I've earned has been sourced with unscrupulous methods. I've intentionally exploited others because the classical definition of work bores me. I rather manipulate people to fill my coffers. I have problems with motivation, self-discipline, perseverance, and responsibility in classical lines of work."

These statements alone should open your eyes to the genuine depth of what defines a psychopath. Sometimes, you have to be blunt to make a point. Not everyone is psychopathic. Some people just have narcissistic traits. Don't diagnose yourself unless a professional undoubtedly diagnoses you.

Considering Facts

Hold your horses before you decide you're a psychopath, because it may just be a trending declaration once people know how psychopathic qualities can be useful. It's much like people claiming to suffer from obsessive-compulsive disorder (OCD). Everyone has a little perfectionism inside of them. This doesn't mean they're all mentally ill. Claiming to have a mental disorder when they don't have one might be a genuine sign that something's sprung loose up there. The trend of claiming to be psychopathic to some extent will keep snowballing as the research on successful psychopaths increases. I'd also love to be relentless and fearless to reach the top of my game, but that doesn't automatically make me murderous. The PCL-R test is fun and informative, but some people I know score around 15, and they're fine. They might be a little narcissistic or unapologetic, but they're harmless.

Before declaring yourself insane, which is an incorrect definition of psychopathy anyway, consider the facts. One theory suggests we have a genetic deficit that doesn't allow us to feel emotions like fear and excitement. It's not that psychopaths are incapable of feeling emotions, either. Psychopathy specialist Adrian Raine, who has 40 years of experience in the field, mentions a nurse named Jane Toppan in his book *The Anatomy of Violence*. Toppan is infamous for killing 31 patients between 1895 and 1901. She would purposely overdose her patients with morphine before watching the light leave their eyes. Toppan was deeply fascinated by the exact moment someone dies. Surprisingly, she was found not guilty and institutionalized until she died at 81.

What makes Toppan's case interesting is what she told her therapists. She'd often reminisce on her crimes to see if she could feel differently about them. She would tell herself that she poisoned her best friend. She poisoned a married couple. She even tried to envision the consequences of what her actions caused the families of her victims. Toppan admitted that she couldn't feel a thing. This is largely due to the disconnection between the prefrontal cortex and amygdala. Emotions are a physiological response in the body. That's why our heart rates increase when we feel scared. Our vital signs even change when we feel deeply saddened by bad news. The disconnection between the two regions in the brain prevents this from happening, albeit many psychopaths show a slight physiological response.

Most psychopaths' heart rates are naturally low, but it's not impossible for them to feel something. Raine believes psychopaths can feel, but it takes a lot more for them to experience emotions. This may also explain their endless pursuit for stimulation. Genetics certainly can predispose anyone to have strong psychopathic tendencies. These people are high-risk triggers, and they will take advantage of people by manipulating the environment. Genetics aside, the environment and experiences can create a psychopath, too. Some people require excellent parenting and the right childhood to suppress their psychopathic side, especially if they have genetic disadvantages. James Fallon, the neuroscientist who tested his brain along with seven of his relatives, is one example of good nurture beating poor genetics.

Fallon calls himself a pro-social psychopath, even after discovering strong evidence of his genetic and neurological predisposition to psychopathy. He might not understand his feelings as well as someone else, but Fallon can certainly be called a successful psychopath. He would never have seen the truth unless the happy accident of his brain scan showed it. However, his relatives weren't surprised, including his mom and wife. That's because it remains challenging for psychopaths to recognize themselves. Chances are that you're not a psychopath if you're questioning yourself as one. You won't easily see it, but the people around you will notice it first, and they might indicate a problem. Fallon didn't see his faults until it was proven.

Once he knew it for a fact, Fallon could list the psychopathic traits he noticed (Shariatmadari, 2016). He explains that he intensively manipulates people around him, and it's something he has to actively fight against. He must be conscious of his habits and traits. He understands how he tries to get others to buy his reality. Fallon is a great example of a genetic or primary psychopath who manages to lead a successful life because he's now conscientious of his problems. This is something he must actively do daily. He wants to remain a pro-social psychopath, and he recognizes how his parents provided him with a life that staved off the environmental factors that could've made him classically psychopathic. This is a huge achievement because psychopaths hardly see the relevance of what others do for them.

Whether you think you're psychopathic, or you're worried about a friend, there are two main facts to consider. First, you're highly unlikely to seek treatment or the truth if you're a psychopath. Rarely do psychopaths spontaneously seek help. They don't evaluate their minds and conscience. Second, you can determine if your loved one is psychopathic by measuring their pulse. Okay, this might be challenging to ask of them, but their pulse could show you whether they have a physiological response to emotions. Their pulse should increase if they fear something. If you worry about being a psychopath, you're probably not one though. Worrying about a friend is different because you can't do this for them. They must become conscientious of their mind first. There are three giveaways that you or someone you know might be a psychopath.

Firstly, if James Fallon teaches us anything, it's that psychopaths are hard to spot, even when you're trying to spot yourself. Many functional or successful psychopaths never question their personalities. They won't recognize their met criteria because of their narcissism and lack of empathy. We only question our actions when we deeply feel our emotions. We may also question them once something happens or someone else mentions them. Otherwise, high-functioning psychopaths don't even notice their personality deficits. They're ignorant, and this makes their life blissful enough not to wonder about other possibilities. The fact that some psychopaths function so well in the broad spectrum of the disorder means many of them will never recognize their faults.

Secondly, psychopaths can secretly struggle with anger and rage for years. A psychopath doesn't have the serotonin kick to cool them down a few minutes after being angered, so they never stop being angry. Instead, they externalize their blame to deal with the anger they carry. They're smart about this though, especially the high-functioning psychopaths. This is where the manipulative and exploitative nature comes from. The clever externalization of their anger could present itself in vengeance or extreme competitiveness. Their anger must go somewhere, after all. Sometimes, the stories they design to redirect people's attention away from them are in retaliation to something that frustrated them. They also don't want people to see their anger because emotions are weaknesses.

Finally, a psychopath can have ethics but they won't have morals. They know where the red tape is, and they know the rules, but they don't care. That's the difference. This also brings another predicament to the table. Knowing the rules but not caring about them means some high-functioning psychopaths might be able to recognize themselves. A psychopath who steers away from criminal behavior might know where the line gets crossed, and they know this could cost them the leadership role they might have. Again, they manipulate the situation enough so they don't cross the line. Well, at least not in a way seen by others. Any behavior that serves their own interests will keep them from crossing the line. Successful psychopaths are intelligent and sly like this.

Nonetheless, you still need a professional diagnosis if you worry about psychopathy in yourself or a loved one. Don't go playing doctor because psychopathy hasn't been researched enough to make definitive conclusions. Knowing the dangers posed by a psychopath and understanding how these can be avoided might keep you and your loved ones safe. That's the ultimate goal, after all. If your goal is to protect your family, then you might not be psychopathic. It would show at least a hint of empathy toward your loved ones.

Conclusion

Psychopaths are indeed wolves hiding among the sheep. They can be sly and unethical, and have no remorse for their inconsiderate or dangerous actions. Encountering one could go unnoticed, and you might even have overlooked your partner's behavior for years. Something made you start questioning the relationship or interactions you have with this person. Perhaps the relationship leaned heavily to one side. You can't understand how selfish someone can be. Let's not even mention the manipulative nature of your good friend. It's either their way or no way. Questioning your relationship with someone is a sign that something isn't right.

Movies and the media have turned psychopaths into these murderous monsters who plot their next kill. We think of them as unscrupulous beings who will hurt anyone they encounter. Psychopaths even become the antiheroes or protagonists of many modern-day movies and series. The more the media creates monsters, the more we believe psychopaths are only cold-blooded killers. It also doesn't work in our favor when our children do questionable things like drowning kittens or dissecting birds. What you know now is that psychopaths are more like the wolves who walk among the sheep. They aren't all wearing masks and wielding chainsaws.

Psychopaths aren't all creatures of tell-tale habits, either. Sometimes, a psychopath can be someone we deeply care for, but they hurt us every chance they get. Sometimes the person we love is so manipulative that we stay with them, even when our warning signals are pinging off the radar. Perhaps you questioned your thoughts because they didn't seem normal. Everyone is allowed a little negativity and unexplained thoughts, but it becomes a potential challenge when it happens so often that we wonder if they're healthy. Psychopaths can be so unemotional that they can hardly ever recognize what they've become.

The only way you find answers is by asking questions. Knowing how psychopaths operate and how they go unnoticed for years can be liberating. It can also protect you and your loved ones from ever becoming victims. One thing we can't deny is that psychopaths don't have the same neurological structures and functions as normal people, so it's okay to suspect everyone. Once you learn how many successful and powerful people are known psychopaths, you have to suspect everyone. Think about Fallon. He never knew about his disorder, which is remarkably strange for a neuroscientist. Look at the presidents we cherish. They were psychopathic. It's what made them unstoppable and determined.

What you've learned in this book will give you the upper hand so that no psychopath can turn you into a victim. We may not understand all the reasons they become violent, and we might not realize how many people are truly psychopathic, but we can use our knowledge of exactly what a psychopath looks like to prevent the worst of interactions. The science behind psychopaths is interesting, but it also helps us discover the creation of this manipulative mind. Their traits can be subtly used to succeed in life, but these same traits are how we recognize them. Their charming personalities will hit a barrier once you understand why and how they use them.

There's no one more self-centered than a psychopath. Sociopaths aren't much different, but some distinct variances could help you determine how dangerous someone can be. You also know where to look for functional psychopaths because they don't end in prison like their criminal counterparts. Moreover, you learned about what triggers a psychopath to cross the line to a dangerous-minded individual. Not every psychopath will rip your intestines out, but some of them are not to be messed with. They have little to no remorse for what happens to you. It won't even bother them, which explains how some psychopaths like Jeffery Dahmer could preserve the bodies of his victims.

It even explains why Norman from the popular *Bates Motel* kept his mom around. Norman knew his mom was dead, but it didn't deter him from dolling her up. His mind was beyond sick, but once again, he fictionally depicts a violent, deadly psychopath. A psychopath's lack of emotional relation is likely the reason they manipulate, hurt, and destroy others, even in the corporate world. You have the questions you need to ask to protect yourself from a friend who may be psychopathic now. You also know how to recognize your child as a psychopath, and you know something can be done to change the outcome of their life.

The latest research in psychiatry also helps you distinguish between sociopaths and psychopaths, which could determine who may or may not stick around. You know how useful therapy is, and you're aware of the potential treatment options evolving for psychopaths. Whether they can be changed or not is a matter of looking at the research. You'll also recognize whether you're a little psychopathic, and you can use the five golden secrets to deal with psychopaths so you don't become a victim of their faulty design.

If this book has taught you anything, I hope you've learned how to protect the people you love and yourself from ever facing off with a psychopath who targets you. There are too many of them in the world to be ignorant of their dangers. You're welcome to leave a comment or review so you can share your experience with me. However, my final piece of advice to you is simple. If you can run, run! Psychopathic natures of any severity can bring you harm, so please run if it's an option. You don't need to surround yourself with people who bring harm to your life. Decide who stays, and remove yourself from the equation of anyone who brings nothing in return.

References

Barker, E. (2016, November 7). *This is how to deal with psychopaths and toxic people: Five proven secrets.* Observer. https://observer.com/2016/11/this-is-how-to-deal-with-psychopaths-and-toxic-people-five-proven-secrets/

Bering, J. (2009, September 29). *The problem with psychopaths: A fearful face doesn't deter them.* Scientific American. https://blogs.scientificamerican.com/bering-in-mind/the-problem-with-psychopaths-a-fearful-face-doesnt-deter-them/

Blonigen, D. M., Hicks, B. M., Krueger, R. F., Patrick, C. J., & Iacono, W. G. (2005). Psychopathic personality traits: Heritability and genetic overlap with internalizing and externalizing psychopathology. *Psychological Medicine, 35*(5), 637–648. https://doi.org/10.1017/s0033291704004180

Bold, K. (2019, October). *Killer instinct.* UC Irvine School of Medicine. http://www.psychiatry.uci.edu/features/fallon-feature-11152013.asp

Bonn, S. A. (2018, January 9). *The differences between psychopaths and sociopaths*. Psychology Today. https://www.psychologytoday.com/ca/blog/wicked-deeds/201801/the-differences-between-psychopaths-and-sociopaths

Bright Side. (2017, September 29). *10 traits of a psychopath*. Bright Side. https://brightside.me/inspiration-health/10-traits-of-a-psychopath-381910/

Bright Side. (2018, February 5). *7 signs that a child will be a psychopath in the future*. Bright Side. https://brightside.me/inspiration-family-and-kids/7-signs-that-a-child-will-be-a-psychopath-in-the-future-444660/

Castillo, H. (2018, March 5). *8 signs your friend is a psychopath*. Girls Chase. https://www.girlschase.com/content/8-signs-your-friend-psychopath

Choi, C. Q. (2009, August 31). *What makes a psychopath? Answers remain elusive*. Live Science. https://www.livescience.com/7859-psychopath-answers-remain-elusive.html

Craparo, G., Schimmenti, A., & Caretti, V. (2013). Traumatic experiences in childhood and psychopathy: A study on a sample of violent offenders from Italy. *European Journal of Psychotraumatology*, *4*(0). https://doi.org/10.3402/ejpt.v4i0.21471

Crossley, L., Woodworth, M., Black, P. J., & Hare, R. (2016). The dark side of negotiation: Examining the outcomes of face-to-face and computer-mediated negotiations among dark personalities. *Personality and Individual Differences*, *91*, 47–51. https://doi.org/10.1016/j.paid.2015.11.052

Decety, J., Chen, C., Harenski, C., & Kiehl, K. A. (2013). An fMRI study of affective perspective taking in individuals with psychopathy: Imagining another in pain does not evoke empathy. *Frontiers in Human Neuroscience*, *7*, 489. https://doi.org/10.3389/fnhum.2013.00489

Delgado, M. (2020, March 24). *Psychopaths – born or made?* Crime Traveller. https://www.crimetraveller.org/2020/03/psychopaths-born-or-made/

Dodgson, L. (2017, August 3). *Both DNA and upbringing can determine whether a child will grow up to be a psychopath — here's how.* Business Insider. https://www.businessinsider.com/how-to-make-a-psychopath-2017-8?IR=T

Drayton, L. A., Santos, L. R., & Baskin-Sommers, A. (2018). Psychopaths fail to automatically take the perspective of others. *Proceedings of the National Academy of Sciences*, *115*(13), 3302–3307. https://doi.org/10.1073/pnas.1721903115

Egan, D. (2016, May 2). *Into the mind of a psychopath.* Discover Magazine.

https://www.discovermagazine.com/mind/into-the-mind-of-a-psychopath

Fox, B., & DeLisi, M. (2019). Psychopathic killers: A meta-analytic review of the psychopathy-homicide nexus. *Aggression and Violent Behavior*, *44*, 67–79. https://doi.org/10.1016/j.avb.2018.11.005

Gao, Y., Raine, A., Chan, F., Venables, P. H., & Mednick, S. A. (2010). Early maternal and paternal bonding, childhood physical abuse and adult psychopathic personality. *Psychological Medicine*, *40*(6), 1007–1016. https://doi.org/10.1017/S0033291709991279

Geddes, L. (2018, May 21). *Can you ever change a violent psychopath's mind?* BBC. https://www.bbc.com/future/article/20180518-can-you-ever-change-a-violent-psychopaths-mind

Hagerty, B. B. (2017, May 16). *When your child is a psychopath.* The Atlantic. https://www.theatlantic.com/magazine/archive/2017/06/when-your-child-is-a-psychopath/524502/

Healthy Place. (2021). *Psychopath test. Am I a psychopath?* Healthy Place. https://www.healthyplace.com/psychological-tests/psychopath-test.-am-i-a-psychopath

Hirstein, W. (2017, June 8). *9 clues that you may be dealing with a psychopath.* Psychology Today. https://www.psychologytoday.com/us/blog/mindmelding/201706/9-clues-you-may-be-dealing-psychopath

Hosking, J. G., Kastman, E. K., Dorfman, H. M., Samanez-Larkin, G. R., Baskin-Sommers, A., Kiehl, K. A., Newman, J. P., & Buckholtz, J. W. (2017). Disrupted prefrontal regulation of striatal subjective value signals in psychopathy. *Neuron, 95*(1), 221-231.e4. https://doi.org/10.1016/j.neuron.2017.06.030

Ishikawa, S. S., Raine, A., Lencz, T., Bihrle, S., & Lacasse, L. (2001). Autonomic stress reactivity and executive functions in successful and unsuccessful criminal psychopaths from the community. *Journal of Abnormal Psychology, 110*(3), 423–432. https://doi.org/10.1037/0021-843x.110.3.423

Jarrett, C. (2016, July 30). *Not all psychopaths are criminal.* Research Digest. https://digest.bps.org.uk/2008/06/26/not-all-psychopaths-are-criminal/

Kane, S. (2018, August 10). *How to recognize a psychopath.* Psych Central. https://psychcentral.com/lib/how-to-recognize-a-psychopath#1

Khan, N. (2018, January 30). *Psychopath vs. sociopath: The telltale signs & difference.* Better Help. https://www.betterhelp.com/advice/sociopathy/psychopath-vs-sociopath-the-telltale-signs-differences/

Kuntz, L. (2021, April 1). *Biden administration plan tackles drug addiction crisis.* Psychiatric Times. https://www.psychiatrictimes.com/view/biden-administration-plan-narrows-in-on-drug-addiction-crisis

Leedom, L. J. (2017). The impact of psychopathy on the family. *Psychopathy - New Updates on an Old Phenomenon.* https://doi.org/10.5772/intechopen.70227

Lindberg, S., & Legg, T. J. (2019, January 9). *Personality disorder: Types, diagnosis and treatment.* Healthline. https://www.healthline.com/health/personality-disorders

Mahmut, M. K., Homewood, J., & Stevenson, R. J. (2008). The characteristics of non-criminals with high psychopathy traits: Are they similar to criminal psychopaths? *Journal of Research in Personality, 42*(3), 679–692. https://doi.org/10.1016/j.jrp.2007.09.002

Martens, W. H. J. (2014). The hidden suffering of the psychopath. *Psychiatric Times, 31*(10). https://www.psychiatrictimes.com/view/hidden-suffering-psychopath

McGreal, S. A. (2018, December 17). *Are murderers unfairly labeled psychopaths?* Psychology Today. https://www.psychologytoday.com/ca/blog/unique-everybody-else/201812/are-murderers-unfairly-labeled-psychopaths

McNeill, B. (2020, May 12). *Not all psychopaths are violent; a new study may explain why some are "successful" instead.* Science Daily. https://www.sciencedaily.com/releases/2020/05/200512190000.htm

McWilliams, S. (2015, November 29). *Not all psychopaths are serial killers - some can function perfectly well in society.* The Journal. https://www.thejournal.ie/readme/psychopathy-2470590-Nov2015/

Morin, A. (2018, April 17). *How to stay mentally strong when you're dealing with a psychopath at work.* Inc. https://www.inc.com/amy-morin/advice-from-a-therapist-5-ways-to-with-a-psychopath-at-work.html

Ni, P. (2018, October 7). *7 characteristics of the modern psychopath.* Psychology Today. https://www.psychologytoday.com/ca/blog/communication-success/201810/7-characteristics-the-modern-psychopath

Psychopaths in Life. (n.d.). *Top 8 vulnerabilities & weaknesses psychopaths & narcissists exploit.*

https://psychopathsinlife.com/vulnerabilities-weaknesses-psychopaths-narcissists-exploit/

Psychotherapy and Counseling. (n.d.). *Self test on psychopathy ("am I a psychopath?" - self assessment, questionnaire)*. https://www.counseling-office.com/surveys/test_psychopathy.phtml

Purse, M., & Block, D. B. (2019). *How sociopaths are different from psychopaths*. Verywell Mind. https://www.verywellmind.com/what-is-a-sociopath-380184

Robinson, K. M. (2014, August 24). *Sociopath vs. psychopath: What's the difference?* WebMD. https://www.webmd.com/mental-health/features/sociopath-psychopath-difference#:~:text=They%20often%20blame%20others%20and

Sandoiu, A., & Collier, J. (2018, May 17). *Psychopathy: What drives pathological selfishness?* Medical News Today. https://www.medicalnewstoday.com/articles/321839

Senju, A., Southgate, V., White, S., & Frith, U. (2009). Mindblind eyes: An absence of spontaneous theory of mind in asperger syndrome. *Science, 325*(5942), 883–885. https://doi.org/10.1126/science.1176170

Shariatmadari, D. (2016, June 29). *Am I a psychopath? You asked Google – here's the answer*. The

Guardian. https://www.theguardian.com/commentisfree/2016/jun/29/am-i-a-psychopath-google-test-psychology-psychiatry-neuroscience

Stillman, J. (2019, September 25). *3 signs you might be a secret psychopath*. Inc. https://www.inc.com/jessica-stillman/3-signs-you-might-be-a-secret-psychopath.html

Tzani-Pepelasi, C. (2018, November 30). *Worried you are dating a psychopath? Signs to look for, according to science*. The Conversation. https://theconversation.com/worried-you-are-dating-a-psychopath-signs-to-look-for-according-to-science-106965

University of Oxford. (2016, August 23). *Presidential candidates may be psychopaths – but that could be a good thing*. Physics. https://phys.org/news/2016-08-presidential-candidates-psychopaths-good.html

Volman, I., Katinka Louise von Borries, A., Hendrik Bulten, B., Jan Verkes, R., Toni, I., & Roelofs, K. (2016). Testosterone modulates altered prefrontal control of emotional actions in psychopathic offenders. *ENeuro*, *3*(1). https://doi.org/10.1523/eneuro.0107-15.2016

Watts, A., & Lilienfeld, S. O. (2016, January 26). *Not all psychopaths are criminals – some psychopathic traits are actually linked to success*. The Conversation.

https://theconversation.com/not-all-psychopaths-are-criminals-some-psychopathic-traits-are-actually-linked-to-success-51282

Yong, E. (2018, March 12). *How psychopaths see the world*. The Atlantic. https://www.theatlantic.com/science/archive/2018/03/a-hidden-problem-at-the-heart-of-psychopathy/555335/